TEACHER'S PET PUBLICATIONS

PUZZLE PACK
for
The Effect of Gamma Rays
on Man in the Moon Marigolds
based on the book by
Paul Zindel

Written by
William T. Collins

© 2005 Teacher's Pet Publications
All Rights Reserved

The materials in this packet are copyrighted
by Teacher's Pet Publications, Inc.

These pages may be duplicated by the purchaser
for use in the purchaser's own classroom.

Copying any of these materials and distributing them
for any other purpose is a violation of the copyright laws.

© 2005 Teacher's Pet Publications, Inc.
www.tpet.com

INTRODUCTION
If you already own the LitPlan for this title, this Puzzle Pack will refresh your Unit Resource Materials and Vocabulary Resource Materials sections plus give you additional materials you can substitute into the tests. If you do not already have a complete LitPlan, these pages will give you some supplemental materials to use with your own plan. There are two main groups of materials: one set for unit words (such as characters' names, symbols, places, etc.) and one set for vocabulary words associated with the book.

WORD LIST
There is a word list for both the unit words and the vocabulary words. These lists show you which words are being used in the materials and the clues or definitions being used for those words. You may want to give students a word list with clues/definitions to help them, or you may want students to only have a word list (without clues/definitions) if you want them to work a little harder. Both are available for duplication. The word lists can also be your "calling key" for the bingo games.

FILL IN THE BLANK AND MATCHING
There are 4 each of the fill in the blank and matching worksheets for both the unit and vocabulary words. These pages can be used either as extra worksheets for students or as objective parts of a unit test. They can be done individually if students need extra help or as a whole class activity to review the material covered.

MAGIC SQUARES
The magic squares not only reinforce the material covered but also work on reasoning and math skills. Many teachers have told us that their students really enjoy doing these!

WORD SEARCH PUZZLES
The word search words go in all directions, as indicated on your answer keys. Two of the word search puzzles have the clues listed rather than the words. This makes the puzzle a little more difficult, but it reinforces the material better. Two word search puzzles have words only for students who find the clue puzzles too difficult.

CROSSWORD PUZZLES
Both unit and vocabulary word sections have 4 crossword puzzles.

BINGO CARDS
There are 32 individual bingo cards for the unit words and 32 individual bingo cards for the vocabulary words. You can use your word list as a "call list," calling the words at random and marking them off of your list as you go, or you could use the flash cards by cutting them apart and drawing the words at random from a hat (or box or whatever). To make a better review, you might ask for the definition and spelling of each word as you call it out–or you could call out the definitions and have students tell you the words they need to look for on the puzzle.

JUGGLE LETTERS
The vocabulary juggle letter game is intended to help students learn the spellings of the words. One sheet has the definitions listed on it as an extra help for students who need it or to reinforce the definitions if you choose to do so.

FLASH CARDS
We've included a set of vocabulary flash cards you can duplicate, cut, and fold for your students. Some teachers make a few sets for general use by the class; others make a set for each student. Some teachers duplicate them for each student and have the students cut & fold their own. You can cut out just the words and put them in a hat, have each student pick out one word and write the definition and a sentence for that word. Students then swap words and papers, with the next student adding a sentence of his own under the last one. You can have students swap as many times as you like. Each time the student will read the sentences written prior to his own and then add a sentence. You can cut out the words and definitions separately and play "I Have; Who Has?" Each student in the room draws a word and definition. The first student says, "I have (the name of the word). Who has the definition?" The student with the definition reads it then says, "I have (the name of the vocabulary word she has). Who has the definition?" The round continues until all words and definitions have been given.

Effect of Gamma Rays Unit Word List

No.	Word	Clue/Definition
1.	ATOM	Small thing that existed since the beginning of the world
2.	BEATRICE	The mother in the book
3.	BEAUTIFUL	Tillie tells her mother, "Mama, you look __!"
4.	BERG	Principal's name: Dr. ____.
5.	BOW	Ruth says Tillie's hair ___ will make people laugh
6.	CAT	Janice Vickery boiled one in a pot
7.	CATARACTS	Nanny has what in her eyes?
8.	CHRIS	Ruth is worried about being embarrassed in front of ___ Burns.
9.	COBALT	Marigold seeds were exposed to ___-60
10.	CONVULSIONS	Ruth's biggest problem is that she has ____.
11.	DAUGHTER	Nanny was left with Beatrice by her ____.
12.	DIFFERENT	Beatrice says the world kills off people who are ____.
13.	DOWNFALL	Beatrice says her ___ started when she married the wrong man
14.	DUTY	Going to the bathroom is Nanny's ____.
15.	EXPERIMENTS	Tillie likes to do them
16.	FAIR	Ruth tells Beatrice that Tillie is one of the finalists in the science ___
17.	GESTAPO	German security police during Nazi regime
18.	GOODMAN	Science teacher
19.	HAND	Part of Tillie's body that came from a star
20.	HANLEY	Gym teacher
21.	HUNSDORFER	Beatrice's last name
22.	HYDROXIDE	Janice boiled the cat in sodium ____ solution.
23.	JANICE	Girl who did the cat project: ____ Vickery
24.	KOOLS	Ruth's favorite cigarettes are ____.
25.	LIPSTICK	Ruth and Beatrice share ___ and cigarettes.
26.	LOON	In high school Beatrice was called Betty the ____.
27.	MARIGOLD	Tillie is raising ____ seeds.
28.	MATILDA	Tillie's real name
29.	MAYO	Ruth has nightmares about Mr. ____.
30.	PAUL	Author: ____ Zindel
31.	PETER	Rabbit's name
32.	RABBIT	Beatrice killed it
33.	RADIOACTIVITY	Mr. Goodman is doing an experiment on ____
34.	RAGGY	What Tillie's slip was
35.	SECRETARY	Ruth is Mr. Goodman's ____.
36.	STAGE	Beatrice is invited to sit there with mothers of the other finalists
37.	TEA	Kind of shop Beatrice wants to open
38.	TICKING	Nanny's movements are like a ____ clock.
39.	WAGON	Beatrice tells Ruth the story of the ___
40.	WORLD	Beatrice told Tillie she hates the ___
41.	ZERO	When Beatrice took stock of her life, she came up with ___

Effect of Gamma Rays Fill In The Blank 1

1. Mr. Goodman is doing an experiment on ____
2. Ruth has nightmares about Mr. ____.
3. Tillie likes to do them
4. Beatrice says her ___ started when she married the wrong man
5. Ruth is worried about being embarrassed in front of ___ Burns.
6. German security police during Nazi regime
7. Beatrice's last name
8. Ruth says Tillie's hair ___ will make people laugh
9. Going to the bathroom is Nanny's ____.
10. Author: ____ Zindel
11. Janice boiled the cat in sodium ____ solution.
12. The mother in the book
13. Janice Vickery boiled one in a pot
14. Beatrice killed it
15. Nanny was left with Beatrice by her ____.
16. Principal's name: Dr. ____.
17. Ruth tells Beatrice that Tillie is one of the finalists in the science ___
18. Beatrice tells Ruth the story of the ___
19. Rabbit's name
20. Ruth and Beatrice share ___ and cigarettes.

Effect of Gamma Rays Fill In The Blank 1 Answer Key

RADIOACTIVITY	1. Mr. Goodman is doing an experiment on ____
MAYO	2. Ruth has nightmares about Mr. ____.
EXPERIMENTS	3. Tillie likes to do them
DOWNFALL	4. Beatrice says her ___ started when she married the wrong man
CHRIS	5. Ruth is worried about being embarrassed in front of ___ Burns.
GESTAPO	6. German security police during Nazi regime
HUNSDORFER	7. Beatrice's last name
BOW	8. Ruth says Tillie's hair ___ will make people laugh
DUTY	9. Going to the bathroom is Nanny's ____.
PAUL	10. Author: ____ Zindel
HYDROXIDE	11. Janice boiled the cat in sodium ____ solution.
BEATRICE	12. The mother in the book
CAT	13. Janice Vickery boiled one in a pot
RABBIT	14. Beatrice killed it
DAUGHTER	15. Nanny was left with Beatrice by her ____.
BERG	16. Principal's name: Dr. ____.
FAIR	17. Ruth tells Beatrice that Tillie is one of the finalists in the science ___
WAGON	18. Beatrice tells Ruth the story of the ___
PETER	19. Rabbit's name
LIPSTICK	20. Ruth and Beatrice share ___ and cigarettes.

Effect of Gamma Rays Fill In The Blank 2

_____
_____
_____
_____
_____
_____
_____
_____
_____
_____
_____
_____
_____
_____
_____
_____
_____
_____
_____
_____

1. Principal's name: Dr. _____.
2. Beatrice is invited to sit there with mothers of the other finalists
3. Tillie is raising _____ seeds.
4. Ruth has nightmares about Mr. _____.
5. When Beatrice took stock of her life, she came up with ___
6. Ruth is worried about being embarrassed in front of ___ Burns.
7. Ruth and Beatrice share ___ and cigarettes.
8. Beatrice says the world kills off people who are _____.
9. What Tillie's slip was
10. Nanny's movements are like a _____ clock.
11. In high school Beatrice was called Betty the _____.
12. Ruth's favorite cigarettes are _____.
13. Small thing that existed since the beginning of the world
14. Nanny has what in her eyes?
15. Beatrice's last name
16. Kind of shop Beatrice wants to open
17. Beatrice says her ___ started when she married the wrong man
18. Janice boiled the cat in sodium _____ solution.
19. Ruth is Mr. Goodman's _____.
20. Ruth's biggest problem is that she has _____.

Effect of Gamma Rays Fill In The Blank 2 Answer Key

BERG	1. Principal's name: Dr. ____.
STAGE	2. Beatrice is invited to sit there with mothers of the other finalists
MARIGOLD	3. Tillie is raising ____ seeds.
MAYO	4. Ruth has nightmares about Mr. ____.
ZERO	5. When Beatrice took stock of her life, she came up with ____
CHRIS	6. Ruth is worried about being embarrassed in front of ___ Burns.
LIPSTICK	7. Ruth and Beatrice share ___ and cigarettes.
DIFFERENT	8. Beatrice says the world kills off people who are ____.
RAGGY	9. What Tillie's slip was
TICKING	10. Nanny's movements are like a ____ clock.
LOON	11. In high school Beatrice was called Betty the ____.
KOOLS	12. Ruth's favorite cigarettes are ____.
ATOM	13. Small thing that existed since the beginning of the world
CATARACTS	14. Nanny has what in her eyes?
HUNSDORFER	15. Beatrice's last name
TEA	16. Kind of shop Beatrice wants to open
DOWNFALL	17. Beatrice says her ___ started when she married the wrong man
HYDROXIDE	18. Janice boiled the cat in sodium ____ solution.
SECRETARY	19. Ruth is Mr. Goodman's ____.
CONVULSIONS	20. Ruth's biggest problem is that she has ____.

Effect of Gamma Rays Fill In The Blank 3

1. Tillie tells her mother, "Mama, you look ___!"
2. Tillie is raising ____ seeds.
3. Nanny's movements are like a ____ clock.
4. What Tillie's slip was
5. Beatrice killed it
6. German security police during Nazi regime
7. Beatrice told Tillie she hates the ___
8. Ruth says Tillie's hair ___ will make people laugh
9. Part of Tillie's body that came from a star
10. Nanny was left with Beatrice by her ____.
11. Beatrice's last name
12. Going to the bathroom is Nanny's ____.
13. Ruth's biggest problem is that she has ____.
14. In high school Beatrice was called Betty the ____.
15. Janice Vickery boiled one in a pot
16. Gym teacher
17. Science teacher
18. Author: ____ Zindel
19. Girl who did the cat project: ____ Vickery
20. Beatrice says the world kills off people who are ____.

Effect of Gamma Rays Fill In The Blank 3 Answer Key

BEAUTIFUL	1. Tillie tells her mother, "Mama, you look ___!"
MARIGOLD	2. Tillie is raising ____ seeds.
TICKING	3. Nanny's movements are like a ____ clock.
RAGGY	4. What Tillie's slip was
RABBIT	5. Beatrice killed it
GESTAPO	6. German security police during Nazi regime
WORLD	7. Beatrice told Tillie she hates the ___
BOW	8. Ruth says Tillie's hair ___ will make people laugh
HAND	9. Part of Tillie's body that came from a star
DAUGHTER	10. Nanny was left with Beatrice by her ____.
HUNSDORFER	11. Beatrice's last name
DUTY	12. Going to the bathroom is Nanny's ____.
CONVULSIONS	13. Ruth's biggest problem is that she has ____.
LOON	14. In high school Beatrice was called Betty the ____.
CAT	15. Janice Vickery boiled one in a pot
HANLEY	16. Gym teacher
GOODMAN	17. Science teacher
PAUL	18. Author: ____ Zindel
JANICE	19. Girl who did the cat project: ____ Vickery
DIFFERENT	20. Beatrice says the world kills off people who are ____.

Effect of Gamma Rays Fill In The Blank 4

1. Principal's name: Dr. _____.
2. The mother in the book
3. Janice Vickery boiled one in a pot
4. Ruth says Tillie's hair ___ will make people laugh
5. Marigold seeds were exposed to ___-60
6. Author: _____ Zindel
7. Beatrice tells Ruth the story of the ___
8. Tillie is raising _____ seeds.
9. What Tillie's slip was
10. Ruth tells Beatrice that Tillie is one of the finalists in the science ___
11. Ruth's biggest problem is that she has _____.
12. Small thing that existed since the beginning of the world
13. Gym teacher
14. Nanny has what in her eyes?
15. Ruth has nightmares about Mr. _____.
16. Ruth's favorite cigarettes are _____.
17. Nanny's movements are like a _____ clock.
18. Going to the bathroom is Nanny's _____.
19. Rabbit's name
20. Beatrice killed it

Effect of Gamma Rays Fill In The Blank 4 Answer Key

BERG	1. Principal's name: Dr. ____.
BEATRICE	2. The mother in the book
CAT	3. Janice Vickery boiled one in a pot
BOW	4. Ruth says Tillie's hair ___ will make people laugh
COBALT	5. Marigold seeds were exposed to ___-60
PAUL	6. Author: ____ Zindel
WAGON	7. Beatrice tells Ruth the story of the ___
MARIGOLD	8. Tillie is raising ____ seeds.
RAGGY	9. What Tillie's slip was
FAIR	10. Ruth tells Beatrice that Tillie is one of the finalists in the science ___
CONVULSIONS	11. Ruth's biggest problem is that she has ____.
ATOM	12. Small thing that existed since the beginning of the world
HANLEY	13. Gym teacher
CATARACTS	14. Nanny has what in her eyes?
MAYO	15. Ruth has nightmares about Mr. ____.
KOOLS	16. Ruth's favorite cigarettes are ____.
TICKING	17. Nanny's movements are like a ____ clock.
DUTY	18. Going to the bathroom is Nanny's ____.
PETER	19. Rabbit's name
RABBIT	20. Beatrice killed it

Effect of Gamma Rays Matching 1

___ 1. TICKING
___ 2. BOW
___ 3. ATOM
___ 4. PETER
___ 5. EXPERIMENTS
___ 6. ZERO
___ 7. BEAUTIFUL
___ 8. BEATRICE
___ 9. KOOLS
___10. MATILDA
___11. HANLEY
___12. DIFFERENT
___13. MARIGOLD
___14. GESTAPO
___15. CAT
___16. RAGGY
___17. TEA
___18. LIPSTICK
___19. MAYO
___20. JANICE
___21. LOON
___22. CONVULSIONS
___23. RABBIT
___24. HUNSDORFER
___25. CHRIS

A. Kind of shop Beatrice wants to open
B. German security police during Nazi regime
C. What Tillie's slip was
D. Tillie is raising ____ seeds.
E. When Beatrice took stock of her life, she came up with ____
F. Rabbit's name
G. Tillie tells her mother, "Mama, you look __!"
H. Ruth's favorite cigarettes are ____.
I. Beatrice killed it
J. Tillie's real name
K. Tillie likes to do them
L. In high school Beatrice was called Betty the ____.
M. Girl who did the cat project: ____ Vickery
N. Janice Vickery boiled one in a pot
O. Ruth's biggest problem is that she has ____.
P. Ruth has nightmares about Mr. ____.
Q. The mother in the book
R. Small thing that existed since the beginning of the world
S. Nanny's movements are like a ____ clock.
T. Ruth says Tillie's hair ___ will make people laugh
U. Ruth is worried about being embarrassed in front of ___ Burns.
V. Beatrice says the world kills off people who are ____.
W. Gym teacher
X. Ruth and Beatrice share ___ and cigarettes.
Y. Beatrice's last name

Effect of Gamma Rays Matching 1 Answer Key

S - 1. TICKING	A. Kind of shop Beatrice wants to open
T - 2. BOW	B. German security police during Nazi regime
R - 3. ATOM	C. What Tillie's slip was
F - 4. PETER	D. Tillie is raising ____ seeds.
K - 5. EXPERIMENTS	E. When Beatrice took stock of her life, she came up with ____
E - 6. ZERO	F. Rabbit's name
G - 7. BEAUTIFUL	G. Tillie tells her mother, "Mama, you look __!"
Q - 8. BEATRICE	H. Ruth's favorite cigarettes are ____.
H - 9. KOOLS	I. Beatrice killed it
J - 10. MATILDA	J. Tillie's real name
W - 11. HANLEY	K. Tillie likes to do them
V - 12. DIFFERENT	L. In high school Beatrice was called Betty the ____.
D - 13. MARIGOLD	M. Girl who did the cat project: ____ Vickery
B - 14. GESTAPO	N. Janice Vickery boiled one in a pot
N - 15. CAT	O. Ruth's biggest problem is that she has ____.
C - 16. RAGGY	P. Ruth has nightmares about Mr. ____.
A - 17. TEA	Q. The mother in the book
X - 18. LIPSTICK	R. Small thing that existed since the beginning of the world
P - 19. MAYO	S. Nanny's movements are like a ____ clock.
M - 20. JANICE	T. Ruth says Tillie's hair ___ will make people laugh
L - 21. LOON	U. Ruth is worried about being embarrassed in front of ___ Burns.
O - 22. CONVULSIONS	V. Beatrice says the world kills off people who are ____.
I - 23. RABBIT	W. Gym teacher
Y - 24. HUNSDORFER	X. Ruth and Beatrice share ___ and cigarettes.
U - 25. CHRIS	Y. Beatrice's last name

Effect of Gamma Rays Matching 2

___ 1. DAUGHTER   A. Nanny was left with Beatrice by her ____.
___ 2. CAT   B. Going to the bathroom is Nanny's ____.
___ 3. COBALT   C. Kind of shop Beatrice wants to open
___ 4. EXPERIMENTS   D. When Beatrice took stock of her life, she came up with ___
___ 5. GOODMAN   E. Marigold seeds were exposed to ___-60
___ 6. LOON   F. Science teacher
___ 7. FAIR   G. In high school Beatrice was called Betty the ____.
___ 8. ZERO   H. Beatrice says her ___ started when she married the wrong man
___ 9. MARIGOLD   I. Janice Vickery boiled one in a pot
___10. HANLEY   J. Tillie likes to do them
___11. RADIOACTIVITY   K. Ruth's biggest problem is that she has ____.
___12. BEATRICE   L. Beatrice tells Ruth the story of the ___
___13. HAND   M. Girl who did the cat project: ____ Vickery
___14. RABBIT   N. The mother in the book
___15. BERG   O. Beatrice says the world kills off people who are ____.
___16. TEA   P. Beatrice killed it
___17. JANICE   Q. Ruth tells Beatrice that Tillie is one of the finalists in the science ___
___18. CONVULSIONS   R. Gym teacher
___19. WAGON   S. Beatrice is invited to sit there with mothers of the other finalists
___20. DIFFERENT   T. Mr. Goodman is doing an experiment on ____
___21. DOWNFALL   U. Principal's name: Dr. ____.
___22. HUNSDORFER   V. Tillie is raising ____ seeds.
___23. DUTY   W. Ruth is Mr. Goodman's ____.
___24. SECRETARY   X. Part of Tillie's body that came from a star
___25. STAGE   Y. Beatrice's last name

Effect of Gamma Rays Matching 2 Answer Key

A - 1. DAUGHTER	A. Nanny was left with Beatrice by her ____.
I - 2. CAT	B. Going to the bathroom is Nanny's ____.
E - 3. COBALT	C. Kind of shop Beatrice wants to open
J - 4. EXPERIMENTS	D. When Beatrice took stock of her life, she came up with ___
F - 5. GOODMAN	E. Marigold seeds were exposed to ___-60
G - 6. LOON	F. Science teacher
Q - 7. FAIR	G. In high school Beatrice was called Betty the ____.
D - 8. ZERO	H. Beatrice says her ___ started when she married the wrong man
V - 9. MARIGOLD	I. Janice Vickery boiled one in a pot
R -10. HANLEY	J. Tillie likes to do them
T -11. RADIOACTIVITY	K. Ruth's biggest problem is that she has ____.
N -12. BEATRICE	L. Beatrice tells Ruth the story of the ___
X -13. HAND	M. Girl who did the cat project: ____ Vickery
P -14. RABBIT	N. The mother in the book
U -15. BERG	O. Beatrice says the world kills off people who are ____.
C -16. TEA	P. Beatrice killed it
M -17. JANICE	Q. Ruth tells Beatrice that Tillie is one of the finalists in the science ___
K -18. CONVULSIONS	R. Gym teacher
L -19. WAGON	S. Beatrice is invited to sit there with mothers of the other finalists
O -20. DIFFERENT	T. Mr. Goodman is doing an experiment on ____
H -21. DOWNFALL	U. Principal's name: Dr. ____.
Y -22. HUNSDORFER	V. Tillie is raising ____ seeds.
B -23. DUTY	W. Ruth is Mr. Goodman's ____.
W -24. SECRETARY	X. Part of Tillie's body that came from a star
S -25. STAGE	Y. Beatrice's last name

Effect of Gamma Rays Matching 3

___ 1. BERG
___ 2. ATOM
___ 3. STAGE
___ 4. WAGON
___ 5. BEATRICE
___ 6. PETER
___ 7. EXPERIMENTS
___ 8. HAND
___ 9. DIFFERENT
___ 10. TICKING
___ 11. BEAUTIFUL
___ 12. RAGGY
___ 13. DAUGHTER
___ 14. RABBIT
___ 15. HANLEY
___ 16. MATILDA
___ 17. DUTY
___ 18. FAIR
___ 19. SECRETARY
___ 20. CAT
___ 21. MAYO
___ 22. ZERO
___ 23. PAUL
___ 24. RADIOACTIVITY
___ 25. BOW

A. Mr. Goodman is doing an experiment on ____
B. When Beatrice took stock of her life, she came up with ___
C. Nanny was left with Beatrice by her ____.
D. Nanny's movements are like a ____ clock.
E. Ruth tells Beatrice that Tillie is one of the finalists in the science ___
F. Tillie tells her mother, "Mama, you look __!"
G. The mother in the book
H. Principal's name: Dr. ____.
I. Tillie likes to do them
J. Beatrice says the world kills off people who are ____.
K. What Tillie's slip was
L. Gym teacher
M. Beatrice is invited to sit there with mothers of the other finalists
N. Ruth says Tillie's hair ___ will make people laugh
O. Going to the bathroom is Nanny's ____.
P. Beatrice killed it
Q. Rabbit's name
R. Janice Vickery boiled one in a pot
S. Author: ____ Zindel
T. Small thing that existed since the beginning of the world
U. Ruth is Mr. Goodman's ____.
V. Part of Tillie's body that came from a star
W. Tillie's real name
X. Beatrice tells Ruth the story of the ___
Y. Ruth has nightmares about Mr. ____.

Effect of Gamma Rays Matching 3 Answer Key

H - 1. BERG	A. Mr. Goodman is doing an experiment on ____
T - 2. ATOM	B. When Beatrice took stock of her life, she came up with ____
M - 3. STAGE	C. Nanny was left with Beatrice by her ____.
X - 4. WAGON	D. Nanny's movements are like a ____ clock.
G - 5. BEATRICE	E. Ruth tells Beatrice that Tillie is one of the finalists in the science ____
Q - 6. PETER	F. Tillie tells her mother, "Mama, you look __!"
I - 7. EXPERIMENTS	G. The mother in the book
V - 8. HAND	H. Principal's name: Dr. ____.
J - 9. DIFFERENT	I. Tillie likes to do them
D - 10. TICKING	J. Beatrice says the world kills off people who are ____.
F - 11. BEAUTIFUL	K. What Tillie's slip was
K - 12. RAGGY	L. Gym teacher
C - 13. DAUGHTER	M. Beatrice is invited to sit there with mothers of the other finalists
P - 14. RABBIT	N. Ruth says Tillie's hair ___ will make people laugh
L - 15. HANLEY	O. Going to the bathroom is Nanny's ____.
W - 16. MATILDA	P. Beatrice killed it
O - 17. DUTY	Q. Rabbit's name
E - 18. FAIR	R. Janice Vickery boiled one in a pot
U - 19. SECRETARY	S. Author: ____ Zindel
R - 20. CAT	T. Small thing that existed since the beginning of the world
Y - 21. MAYO	U. Ruth is Mr. Goodman's ____.
B - 22. ZERO	V. Part of Tillie's body that came from a star
S - 23. PAUL	W. Tillie's real name
A - 24. RADIOACTIVITY	X. Beatrice tells Ruth the story of the ___
N - 25. BOW	Y. Ruth has nightmares about Mr. ____.

Effect of Gamma Rays Matching 4

___ 1. BERG
___ 2. GESTAPO
___ 3. MATILDA
___ 4. EXPERIMENTS
___ 5. CATARACTS
___ 6. DUTY
___ 7. PETER
___ 8. BEAUTIFUL
___ 9. MAYO
___10. KOOLS
___11. JANICE
___12. RABBIT
___13. BOW
___14. ATOM
___15. WORLD
___16. DIFFERENT
___17. PAUL
___18. TICKING
___19. FAIR
___20. BEATRICE
___21. GOODMAN
___22. CONVULSIONS
___23. LOON
___24. RAGGY
___25. STAGE

A. In high school Beatrice was called Betty the ____.
B. Beatrice told Tillie she hates the ___
C. Nanny has what in her eyes?
D. Ruth tells Beatrice that Tillie is one of the finalists in the science ___
E. Beatrice says the world kills off people who are ____.
F. Science teacher
G. Tillie's real name
H. Principal's name: Dr. ____.
I. Ruth's favorite cigarettes are ____.
J. Ruth says Tillie's hair ___ will make people laugh
K. Ruth has nightmares about Mr. ____.
L. Small thing that existed since the beginning of the world
M. Nanny's movements are like a ____ clock.
N. What Tillie's slip was
O. Rabbit's name
P. Beatrice killed it
Q. German security police during Nazi regime
R. Tillie likes to do them
S. Author: ____ Zindel
T. Ruth's biggest problem is that she has ____.
U. Beatrice is invited to sit there with mothers of the other finalists
V. The mother in the book
W. Going to the bathroom is Nanny's ____.
X. Tillie tells her mother, "Mama, you look __!"
Y. Girl who did the cat project: ____ Vickery

Effect of Gamma Rays Matching 4 Answer Key

H - 1. BERG	A.	In high school Beatrice was called Betty the ____.
Q - 2. GESTAPO	B.	Beatrice told Tillie she hates the ___
G - 3. MATILDA	C.	Nanny has what in her eyes?
R - 4. EXPERIMENTS	D.	Ruth tells Beatrice that Tillie is one of the finalists in the science ___
C - 5. CATARACTS	E.	Beatrice says the world kills off people who are ____.
W - 6. DUTY	F.	Science teacher
O - 7. PETER	G.	Tillie's real name
X - 8. BEAUTIFUL	H.	Principal's name: Dr. ____.
K - 9. MAYO	I.	Ruth's favorite cigarettes are ____.
I - 10. KOOLS	J.	Ruth says Tillie's hair ___ will make people laugh
Y - 11. JANICE	K.	Ruth has nightmares about Mr. ____.
P - 12. RABBIT	L.	Small thing that existed since the beginning of the world
J - 13. BOW	M.	Nanny's movements are like a ____ clock.
L - 14. ATOM	N.	What Tillie's slip was
B - 15. WORLD	O.	Rabbit's name
E - 16. DIFFERENT	P.	Beatrice killed it
S - 17. PAUL	Q.	German security police during Nazi regime
M - 18. TICKING	R.	Tillie likes to do them
D - 19. FAIR	S.	Author: ____ Zindel
V - 20. BEATRICE	T.	Ruth's biggest problem is that she has ____.
F - 21. GOODMAN	U.	Beatrice is invited to sit there with mothers of the other finalists
T - 22. CONVULSIONS	V.	The mother in the book
A - 23. LOON	W.	Going to the bathroom is Nanny's ____.
N - 24. RAGGY	X.	Tillie tells her mother, "Mama, you look __!"
U - 25. STAGE	Y.	Girl who did the cat project: ____ Vickery

Effect of Gamma Rays Magic Squares 1

Match the definition with the vocabulary word. Put your answers in the magic squares below. When your answers are correct, all columns and rows will add to the same number.

A. ATOM
B. COBALT
C. CHRIS
D. LOON
E. DAUGHTER
F. ZERO
G. EXPERIMENTS
H. HANLEY
I. DUTY
J. WAGON
K. GOODMAN
L. CAT
M. DIFFERENT
N. KOOLS
O. MARIGOLD
P. JANICE

1. Small thing that existed since the beginning of the world
2. Ruth's favorite cigarettes are ____.
3. Beatrice tells Ruth the story of the ____
4. Nanny was left with Beatrice by her ____.
5. Tillie likes to do them
6. Janice Vickery boiled one in a pot
7. Girl who did the cat project: ____ Vickery
8. Ruth is worried about being embarrassed in front of ___ Burns.
9. Tillie is raising ____ seeds.
10. In high school Beatrice was called Betty the ____.
11. Gym teacher
12. Science teacher
13. Going to the bathroom is Nanny's ____.
14. When Beatrice took stock of her life, she came up with ___
15. Marigold seeds were exposed to ___-60
16. Beatrice says the world kills off people who are ____.

A=	B=	C=	D=
E=	F=	G=	H=
I=	J=	K=	L=
M=	N=	O=	P=

Effect of Gamma Rays Magic Squares 1 Answer Key

Match the definition with the vocabulary word. Put your answers in the magic squares below. When your answers are correct, all columns and rows will add to the same number.

A. ATOM
B. COBALT
C. CHRIS
D. LOON
E. DAUGHTER
F. ZERO
G. EXPERIMENTS
H. HANLEY
I. DUTY
J. WAGON
K. GOODMAN
L. CAT
M. DIFFERENT
N. KOOLS
O. MARIGOLD
P. JANICE

1. Small thing that existed since the beginning of the world
2. Ruth's favorite cigarettes are ____.
3. Beatrice tells Ruth the story of the ___
4. Nanny was left with Beatrice by her ____.
5. Tillie likes to do them
6. Janice Vickery boiled one in a pot
7. Girl who did the cat project: ____ Vickery
8. Ruth is worried about being embarrassed in front of ___ Burns.
9. Tillie is raising ____ seeds.
10. In high school Beatrice was called Betty the ____.
11. Gym teacher
12. Science teacher
13. Going to the bathroom is Nanny's ____.
14. When Beatrice took stock of her life, she came up with ___
15. Marigold seeds were exposed to ___-60
16. Beatrice says the world kills off people who are ____.

A=1	B=15	C=8	D=10
E=4	F=14	G=5	H=11
I=13	J=3	K=12	L=6
M=16	N=2	O=9	P=7

Effect of Gamma Rays Magic Squares 2

Match the definition with the vocabulary word. Put your answers in the magic squares below. When your answers are correct, all columns and rows will add to the same number.

A. MAYO
B. EXPERIMENTS
C. FAIR
D. BEAUTIFUL
E. LIPSTICK
F. HAND
G. LOON
H. JANICE
I. MATILDA
J. CONVULSIONS
K. SECRETARY
L. RAGGY
M. DIFFERENT
N. GESTAPO
O. ATOM
P. ZERO

1. Small thing that existed since the beginning of the world
2. Tillie tells her mother, "Mama, you look __!"
3. Ruth's biggest problem is that she has ____.
4. Ruth and Beatrice share ___ and cigarettes.
5. Tillie's real name
6. Part of Tillie's body that came from a star
7. When Beatrice took stock of her life, she came up with ___
8. Ruth tells Beatrice that Tillie is one of the finalists in the science ___
9. Girl who did the cat project: ____ Vickery
10. Ruth is Mr. Goodman's ____.
11. Ruth has nightmares about Mr. ____.
12. German security police during Nazi regime
13. Tillie likes to do them
14. Beatrice says the world kills off people who are ____.
15. In high school Beatrice was called Betty the ____.
16. What Tillie's slip was

A=	B=	C=	D=
E=	F=	G=	H=
I=	J=	K=	L=
M=	N=	O=	P=

Effect of Gamma Rays Magic Squares 2 Answer Key

Match the definition with the vocabulary word. Put your answers in the magic squares below. When your answers are correct, all columns and rows will add to the same number.

A. MAYO
B. EXPERIMENTS
C. FAIR
D. BEAUTIFUL
E. LIPSTICK
F. HAND
G. LOON
H. JANICE
I. MATILDA
J. CONVULSIONS
K. SECRETARY
L. RAGGY
M. DIFFERENT
N. GESTAPO
O. ATOM
P. ZERO

1. Small thing that existed since the beginning of the world
2. Tillie tells her mother, "Mama, you look __!"
3. Ruth's biggest problem is that she has ____.
4. Ruth and Beatrice share ___ and cigarettes.
5. Tillie's real name
6. Part of Tillie's body that came from a star
7. When Beatrice took stock of her life, she came up with ___
8. Ruth tells Beatrice that Tillie is one of the finalists in the science ___
9. Girl who did the cat project: ____ Vickery
10. Ruth is Mr. Goodman's ____.
11. Ruth has nightmares about Mr. ____.
12. German security police during Nazi regime
13. Tillie likes to do them
14. Beatrice says the world kills off people who are ____.
15. In high school Beatrice was called Betty the ____.
16. What Tillie's slip was

A=11	B=13	C=8	D=2
E=4	F=6	G=15	H=9
I=5	J=3	K=10	L=16
M=14	N=12	O=1	P=7

Effect of Gamma Rays Magic Squares 3

Match the definition with the vocabulary word. Put your answers in the magic squares below. When your answers are correct, all columns and rows will add to the same number.

A. CAT
B. DIFFERENT
C. BOW
D. TEA
E. STAGE
F. LIPSTICK
G. LOON
H. GOODMAN
I. DUTY
J. GESTAPO
K. ATOM
L. KOOLS
M. JANICE
N. HAND
O. COBALT
P. TICKING

1. Science teacher
2. Girl who did the cat project: ____ Vickery
3. Beatrice says the world kills off people who are ____.
4. Small thing that existed since the beginning of the world
5. German security police during Nazi regime
6. Ruth says Tillie's hair ____ will make people laugh
7. Nanny's movements are like a ____ clock.
8. Beatrice is invited to sit there with mothers of the other finalists
9. Marigold seeds were exposed to ____-60
10. Ruth and Beatrice share ____ and cigarettes.
11. Going to the bathroom is Nanny's ____.
12. Kind of shop Beatrice wants to open
13. Janice Vickery boiled one in a pot
14. Ruth's favorite cigarettes are ____.
15. In high school Beatrice was called Betty the ____.
16. Part of Tillie's body that came from a star

A=	B=	C=	D=
E=	F=	G=	H=
I=	J=	K=	L=
M=	N=	O=	P=

Effect of Gamma Rays Magic Squares 3 Answer Key

Match the definition with the vocabulary word. Put your answers in the magic squares below. When your answers are correct, all columns and rows will add to the same number.

A. CAT
B. DIFFERENT
C. BOW
D. TEA
E. STAGE
F. LIPSTICK
G. LOON
H. GOODMAN
I. DUTY
J. GESTAPO
K. ATOM
L. KOOLS
M. JANICE
N. HAND
O. COBALT
P. TICKING

1. Science teacher
2. Girl who did the cat project: ____ Vickery
3. Beatrice says the world kills off people who are ____.
4. Small thing that existed since the beginning of the world
5. German security police during Nazi regime
6. Ruth says Tillie's hair ___ will make people laugh
7. Nanny's movements are like a ____ clock.
8. Beatrice is invited to sit there with mothers of the other finalists
9. Marigold seeds were exposed to ___-60
10. Ruth and Beatrice share ___ and cigarettes.
11. Going to the bathroom is Nanny's ____.
12. Kind of shop Beatrice wants to open
13. Janice Vickery boiled one in a pot
14. Ruth's favorite cigarettes are ____.
15. In high school Beatrice was called Betty the ____.
16. Part of Tillie's body that came from a star

A=13	B=3	C=6	D=12
E=8	F=10	G=15	H=1
I=11	J=5	K=4	L=14
M=2	N=16	O=9	P=7

Effect of Gamma Rays Magic Squares 4

Match the definition with the vocabulary word. Put your answers in the magic squares below. When your answers are correct, all columns and rows will add to the same number.

A. MARIGOLD
B. BERG
C. RADIOACTIVITY
D. BOW
E. HAND
F. WORLD
G. DAUGHTER
H. RAGGY
I. DOWNFALL
J. CHRIS
K. FAIR
L. ZERO
M. WAGON
N. TICKING
O. SECRETARY
P. BEATRICE

1. Beatrice tells Ruth the story of the ___
2. Beatrice told Tillie she hates the ___
3. What Tillie's slip was
4. Ruth is Mr. Goodman's ___.
5. When Beatrice took stock of her life, she came up with ___
6. Mr. Goodman is doing an experiment on ___
7. Tillie is raising ___ seeds.
8. Ruth is worried about being embarrassed in front of ___ Burns.
9. Ruth tells Beatrice that Tillie is one of the finalists in the science ___
10. Ruth says Tillie's hair ___ will make people laugh
11. Principal's name: Dr. ___.
12. Beatrice says her ___ started when she married the wrong man
13. Nanny's movements are like a ___ clock.
14. Part of Tillie's body that came from a star
15. Nanny was left with Beatrice by her ___.
16. The mother in the book

A=	B=	C=	D=
E=	F=	G=	H=
I=	J=	K=	L=
M=	N=	O=	P=

Effect of Gamma Rays Magic Squares 4 Answer Key

Match the definition with the vocabulary word. Put your answers in the magic squares below. When your answers are correct, all columns and rows will add to the same number.

A. MARIGOLD
B. BERG
C. RADIOACTIVITY
D. BOW
E. HAND
F. WORLD

G. DAUGHTER
H. RAGGY
I. DOWNFALL
J. CHRIS
K. FAIR
L. ZERO

M. WAGON
N. TICKING
O. SECRETARY
P. BEATRICE

1. Beatrice tells Ruth the story of the ___
2. Beatrice told Tillie she hates the ___
3. What Tillie's slip was
4. Ruth is Mr. Goodman's ___.
5. When Beatrice took stock of her life, she came up with ___
6. Mr. Goodman is doing an experiment on ___
7. Tillie is raising ___ seeds.
8. Ruth is worried about being embarrassed in front of ___ Burns.
9. Ruth tells Beatrice that Tillie is one of the finalists in the science ___
10. Ruth says Tillie's hair ___ will make people laugh
11. Principal's name: Dr. ___.
12. Beatrice says her ___ started when she married the wrong man
13. Nanny's movements are like a ___ clock.
14. Part of Tillie's body that came from a star
15. Nanny was left with Beatrice by her ___.
16. The mother in the book

A=7	B=11	C=6	D=10
E=14	F=2	G=15	H=3
I=12	J=8	K=9	L=5
M=1	N=13	O=4	P=16

Effect of Gamma Rays Word Search 1

```
P S N C B E A T R I C E O W R L H S
E E Z O A W M W I K F P B T A F K B
T C B B R T N A L C A J W B C G M D
E R H A V T L U T T K Q C W A N O K
R E Z L R Y F K S I N I N Z T W D N
K T K T W I J E V E L F N S A W I V
S A R C T A G T D W W D M G R Q F H
B R P U N D W I C W H S A L A E F X
K Y A I Z W X Z H H N H G O C G E P
V E C X E O B H R O A U A O T A R G
B E R G R A B B I T R N P N S T E A
H C Y D O C O S S I A S D A L S N C
Z D Y J Y W L R A M D D H V U E T C
M H S C Y U K F D R M O A C J L Y R
Q A J L V P W O R L D R Y T U D G W
B T Y N L F O V O D W F X W O Z G R
V C O O T G Q T T L J E M V H M A H
Q C M A R I G O L D S R X N R H R B
```

Author: ____ Zindel (4)
Beatrice is invited to sit there with mothers of the other finalists (5)
Beatrice killed it (6)
Beatrice says the world kills off people who are ____. (9)
Beatrice tells Ruth the story of the ___ (5)
Beatrice told Tillie she hates the ___ (5)
Beatrice's last name (10)
German security police during Nazi regime (7)
Girl who did the cat project: ____ Vickery (6)
Going to the bathroom is Nanny's ____. (4)
Gym teacher (6)
In high school Beatrice was called Betty the ____. (4)
Janice Vickery boiled one in a pot (3)
Janice boiled the cat in sodium ____ solution. (9)
Kind of shop Beatrice wants to open (3)
Marigold seeds were exposed to ___-60 (6)
Nanny has what in her eyes? (9)
Nanny's movements are like a ____ clock. (7)
Part of Tillie's body that came from a star (4)
Principal's name: Dr. ____. (4)
Rabbit's name (5)
Ruth has nightmares about Mr. ____. (4)
Ruth is Mr. Goodman's ____. (9)
Ruth is worried about being embarrassed in front of ___ Burns. (5)
Ruth says Tillie's hair ___ will make people laugh (3)
Ruth tells Beatrice that Tillie is one of the finalists in the science ___ (4)
Ruth's biggest problem is that she has ____. (11)
Ruth's favorite cigarettes are ____. (5)
Science teacher (7)
Small thing that existed since the beginning of the world (4)
The mother in the book (8)
Tillie is raising ____ seeds. (8)
Tillie tells her mother, "Mama, you look __!" (9)
Tillie's real name (7)
What Tillie's slip was (5)
When Beatrice took stock of her life, she came up with ___ (4)

Effect of Gamma Rays Word Search 1 Answer Key

```
P  S     C  B  E─A─T─R─I─C─E  O  W
E  E     O  A     M     I     P     A
T  C     B  L     T  A  C  A        C  G
E  R     A  L     U  T  K           A     O
R  E     L        F  S  I           T        D  N
   T        I  J  E     E  L        A           I
   A     T  A  G  I  C           G           E  F
   R  U  N  Z  X  H  N  H  S  A  L  A     G  F
   Y  A  I  E  O     R  O  A  O     A  C  A  E
B  E  R  G  R  A  B  B  I  T  R  N  P  N  S  T  A
   Y     D  O  O  S  S  I  A  S  D  A     S  E
      M  H  W  L  F  A  M     D     U  L     N
         A  U  K  O  R  L  D  O  A  T  U  D  T
         Y  V  W  O        R  F        O     Y
         O  N  O  G        L  E           M  G
      C  M  A  R  I  G  O  L  D  S  R        A  R
```

Author: ____ Zindel (4)
Beatrice is invited to sit there with mothers of the other finalists (5)
Beatrice killed it (6)
Beatrice says the world kills off people who are ____. (9)
Beatrice tells Ruth the story of the ____ (5)
Beatrice told Tillie she hates the ____ (5)
Beatrice's last name (10)
German security police during Nazi regime (7)
Girl who did the cat project: ____ Vickery (6)
Going to the bathroom is Nanny's ____. (4)
Gym teacher (6)
In high school Beatrice was called Betty the ____. (4)
Janice Vickery boiled one in a pot (3)
Janice boiled the cat in sodium ____ solution. (9)
Kind of shop Beatrice wants to open (3)
Marigold seeds were exposed to ____-60 (6)
Nanny has what in her eyes? (9)
Nanny's movements are like a ____ clock. (7)
Part of Tillie's body that came from a star (4)
Principal's name: Dr. ____. (4)
Rabbit's name (5)
Ruth has nightmares about Mr. ____. (4)
Ruth is Mr. Goodman's ____. (9)
Ruth is worried about being embarrassed in front of ____ Burns. (5)
Ruth says Tillie's hair ____ will make people laugh (3)
Ruth tells Beatrice that Tillie is one of the finalists in the science ____ (4)
Ruth's biggest problem is that she has ____. (11)
Ruth's favorite cigarettes are ____. (5)
Science teacher (7)
Small thing that existed since the beginning of the world (4)
The mother in the book (8)
Tillie is raising ____ seeds. (8)
Tillie tells her mother, "Mama, you look ____!" (9)
Tillie's real name (7)
What Tillie's slip was (5)
When Beatrice took stock of her life, she came up with ____ (4)

Effect of Gamma Rays Word Search 2

```
M A Y O B T B H G R P Z E R O W B Q
M A T I L D A E U G M V Z X O E D R
D Z R S N N P N A N K W N B A T B T
J U K I L V A X F T S F Z U P J H V
J N T E G M U X X L R D T K T X D K
A R Y Y D O L N W L R I O Q P N I L
T A F O L W L F R D F O C R S B F G
O G O C L N D D H U L H Y E F R F M
M G B D A C K H L S R V Z G I E E V
C Y E J F T G Y V I K J C A H D R G
O W R G N N A D S M L G F P P W E S
B W G W W Y M R O D I O J P K D N X
A S L Z O R P O A D P P Q F E K T L
L N K X D R P X B C S A W Q C T Q Y
T H N X W K L I B L T T H A Y M E N
J A N I C E H D I P I S T A G E O R
T I C K I N G E T Y C E E G N O K N
S E C R E T A R Y N K G A L L D N Y
```

Author: ____ Zindel (4)
Beatrice is invited to sit there with mothers of the other finalists (5)
Beatrice killed it (6)
Beatrice says her ___ started when she married the wrong man (8)
Beatrice says the world kills off people who are ____. (9)
Beatrice tells Ruth the story of the ___ (5)
Beatrice told Tillie she hates the ___ (5)
Beatrice's last name (10)
German security police during Nazi regime (7)
Girl who did the cat project: ____ Vickery (6)
Going to the bathroom is Nanny's ____. (4)
Gym teacher (6)
In high school Beatrice was called Betty the ____. (4)
Janice Vickery boiled one in a pot (3)
Janice boiled the cat in sodium ____ solution. (9)
Kind of shop Beatrice wants to open (3)
Marigold seeds were exposed to ___-60 (6)
Nanny has what in her eyes? (9)
Nanny's movements are like a ____ clock.

(7)
Part of Tillie's body that came from a star (4)
Principal's name: Dr. ____. (4)
Rabbit's name (5)
Ruth and Beatrice share ___ and cigarettes. (8)
Ruth has nightmares about Mr. ____. (4)
Ruth is Mr. Goodman's ____. (9)
Ruth is worried about being embarrassed in front of ___ Burns. (5)
Ruth says Tillie's hair ___ will make people laugh (3)
Ruth tells Beatrice that Tillie is one of the finalists in the science ___ (4)
Ruth's favorite cigarettes are ____. (5)
Science teacher (7)
Small thing that existed since the beginning of the world (4)
The mother in the book (8)
Tillie is raising ____ seeds. (8)
Tillie tells her mother, "Mama, you look __!"(9)
Tillie's real name (7)
What Tillie's slip was (5)
When Beatrice took stock of her life, she came up with ___ (4)

Effect of Gamma Rays Word Search 2 Answer Key

```
M  A  Y  O        B  H              Z  E  R  O  W  B
M  A  T  I  L  D  A  E  U              O     E
D     R        N  P  N  A           B     A
      U           I  A     T  S     U
         T  E  G  M  U        R  D  T  K        D
A  R  Y  Y  D  O  L           I  O           I
T  A     O  L     L        F  O  C  R        F
O  G  O  C  L        D  U  L  H     E  F  R  F
M  G  B     A        H  L  S  R        I  E  E
C  Y  E     F  T     Y                 A     R
O     R        N  A  D  S     L     F        E
B     G  W  W        R  R     I     O  P     N
A                 O        O  A     P  P     E
L              D  R        X  B  C  S  A  W  C  T
T                    L  I  B     T  H  A     E  N
   J  A  N  I  C  E     D  I     I  S  T  A  G  E  O  R
T  I  C  K  I  N  G  E  T     C  E  E     N  O
S  E  C  R  E  T  A  R  Y        K  G  A     L  D  N
```

Author: ____ Zindel (4)
Beatrice is invited to sit there with mothers of the other finalists (5)
Beatrice killed it (6)
Beatrice says her ___ started when she married the wrong man (8)
Beatrice says the world kills off people who are ____. (9)
Beatrice tells Ruth the story of the ___ (5)
Beatrice told Tillie she hates the ___ (5)
Beatrice's last name (10)
German security police during Nazi regime (7)
Girl who did the cat project: ____ Vickery (6)
Going to the bathroom is Nanny's ____. (4)
Gym teacher (6)
In high school Beatrice was called Betty the ____. (4)
Janice Vickery boiled one in a pot (3)
Janice boiled the cat in sodium ____ solution. (9)
Kind of shop Beatrice wants to open (3)
Marigold seeds were exposed to ___-60 (6)
Nanny has what in her eyes? (9)
Nanny's movements are like a ____ clock.

(7)
Part of Tillie's body that came from a star (4)
Principal's name: Dr. ____. (4)
Rabbit's name (5)
Ruth and Beatrice share ___ and cigarettes. (8)
Ruth has nightmares about Mr. ____. (4)
Ruth is Mr. Goodman's ____. (9)
Ruth is worried about being embarrassed in front of ___ Burns. (5)
Ruth says Tillie's hair ___ will make people laugh (3)
Ruth tells Beatrice that Tillie is one of the finalists in the science ___ (4)
Ruth's favorite cigarettes are ____. (5)
Science teacher (7)
Small thing that existed since the beginning of the world (4)
The mother in the book (8)
Tillie is raising ____ seeds. (8)
Tillie tells her mother, "Mama, you look __!" (9)
Tillie's real name (7)
What Tillie's slip was (5)
When Beatrice took stock of her life, she came up with ___ (4)

Effect of Gamma Rays Word Search 3

```
Z S Q Y L R C C S P H C Q K K K L Y W S
G T B P M B K A F B A H S F J G O Z O M
G A X Z R H E T D D N R A D Z M M O R R
X G H S N O G A W E D I X O R D Y H L L
N E G X M L U R T L R S P A U K N L D S
R A V M U G X A J R Q S B T S J A S P S
T T W A H S R C A F I B Y L L F P L E J
K O P T C E A T N R I C A R N O B B T W
B M E A O C G S I T X E E W Y R O E E X
B R T Q B R G C C S T F O A B E H N R S
B K C K A E Y M E M R D M R E Z C L M G
D N O X L T F S K O Y L E A A X V I A K
Z C N L T A W T D B E O X D U N Q P T N
H T V G C R G S S D L G P I T N N S I S
S L U Y C Y N O Z Y N I E O I G D T L S
S D L L M U V B O I A R R A F V M I D L
R S S C H W N K K D H A I C U Z C C A G
X T I H G W F C H I M M M T L N J K H R
B Y O Y E H I H W F Q A E I N Y F R W Q
C R N X S T V L V F W N N V S F M D W D
D H S W T H J W K E H T T I D F Q P N L
F F P Z A N Q W L R H N S T L R C Y M V
T Z T S P S Q D R E H F Z Y F R X B T T
Q Z H L O F Q H V N G V Q Z S M D Z Z V
W R J B T H N R J T X R Y M N X D Q Y W
```

ATOM	EXPERIMENTS	MAYO
BEATRICE	FAIR	PAUL
BEAUTIFUL	GESTAPO	PETER
BERG	GOODMAN	RABBIT
BOW	HAND	RADIOACTIVITY
CAT	HANLEY	RAGGY
CATARACTS	HUNSDORFER	SECRETARY
CHRIS	HYDROXIDE	STAGE
COBALT	JANICE	TEA
CONVULSIONS	KOOLS	TICKING
DAUGHTER	LIPSTICK	WAGON
DIFFERENT	LOON	WORLD
DOWNFALL	MARIGOLD	ZERO
DUTY	MATILDA	

Effect of Gamma Rays Word Search 3 Answer Key

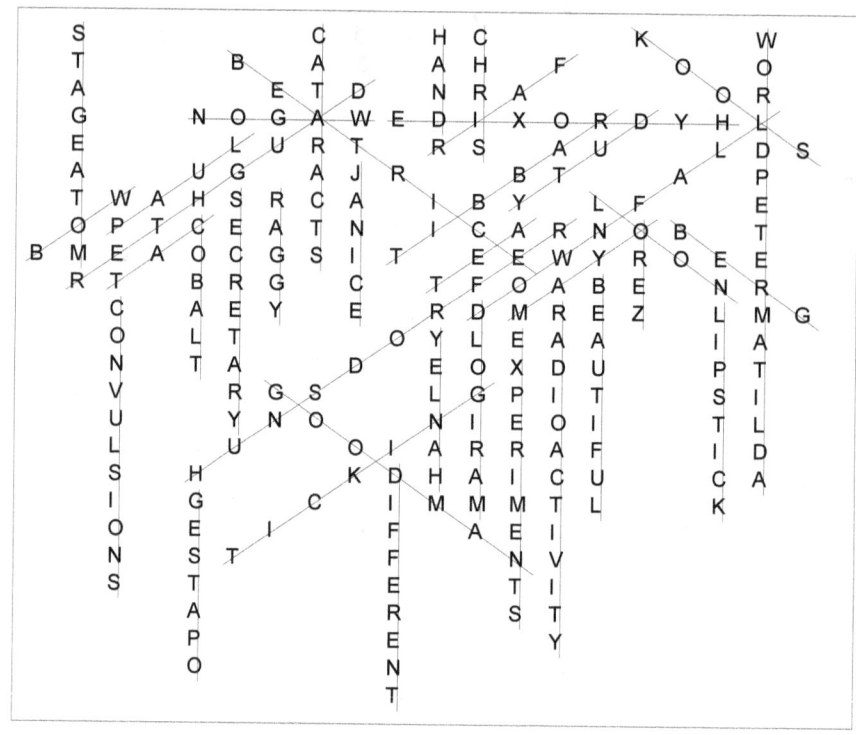

ATOM	EXPERIMENTS	MAYO
BEATRICE	FAIR	PAUL
BEAUTIFUL	GESTAPO	PETER
BERG	GOODMAN	RABBIT
BOW	HAND	RADIOACTIVITY
CAT	HANLEY	RAGGY
CATARACTS	HUNSDORFER	SECRETARY
CHRIS	HYDROXIDE	STAGE
COBALT	JANICE	TEA
CONVULSIONS	KOOLS	TICKING
DAUGHTER	LIPSTICK	WAGON
DIFFERENT	LOON	WORLD
DOWNFALL	MARIGOLD	ZERO
DUTY	MATILDA	

Effect of Gamma Rays Word Search 4

```
K D V P E W G L H D Y K W M C B G W V L
N W B C F X R K O L E W M A H B P D C V
S Z Z A K R P G N O L R K Y W G N R J L
B E A T R I C E C I N A J O C O B A L T
M E C V M R P S R N A F B J G Z T Z P T
A Y A R W A R T W I H R M A E N K W I V
T F K U E E H A P T M D W R M M M C M W
I M P M T T Z P H P W E O L W C K T V V
L Z Q E S I A O R A D W N W A I T L G M
D V P T T X F R C H N D S T N D G B T K
A K M J A K K U Y D R D A G S F R P C D
C C Q C G G G L Q H R F B Q P A S W Z
H O N P E V F B T L A N H A V Z A L Y C
R D N M B W Q X G C F X M F I Z H U L C
I U O V L S G V T T J B D M M R U H L T
S T W G U Z S S D A U G H T E R N Y I M
A Y O O M L M L P D V V Z M D A S D P Y
N T R O Y M S V K K F F Y A I G D R S R
L T L D Q M X I L D J H M R F G O O T R
V Y D M W J T F O G C S J I F Y R X I R
R J B A V I Z P R N L Y H G E T F I C L
N R T N B R F E P O S Y G O R S E D K M
P L K B Q V B R O S T J T L E D R E W R
S V A Q V H C K M Y H S V D N R L L Z V
G R Y R A D I O A C T I V I T Y D F H B
```

ATOM

BEATRICE

BEAUTIFUL

BERG

BOW

CAT

CATARACTS

CHRIS

COBALT

CONVULSIONS

DAUGHTER

DIFFERENT

DOWNFALL

DUTY

EXPERIMENTS

FAIR

GESTAPO

GOODMAN

HAND

HANLEY

HUNSDORFER

HYDROXIDE

JANICE

KOOLS

LIPSTICK

LOON

MARIGOLD

MATILDA

MAYO

PAUL

PETER

RABBIT

RADIOACTIVITY

RAGGY

SECRETARY

STAGE

TEA

TICKING

WAGON

WORLD

ZERO

Effect of Gamma Rays Word Search 4 Answer Key

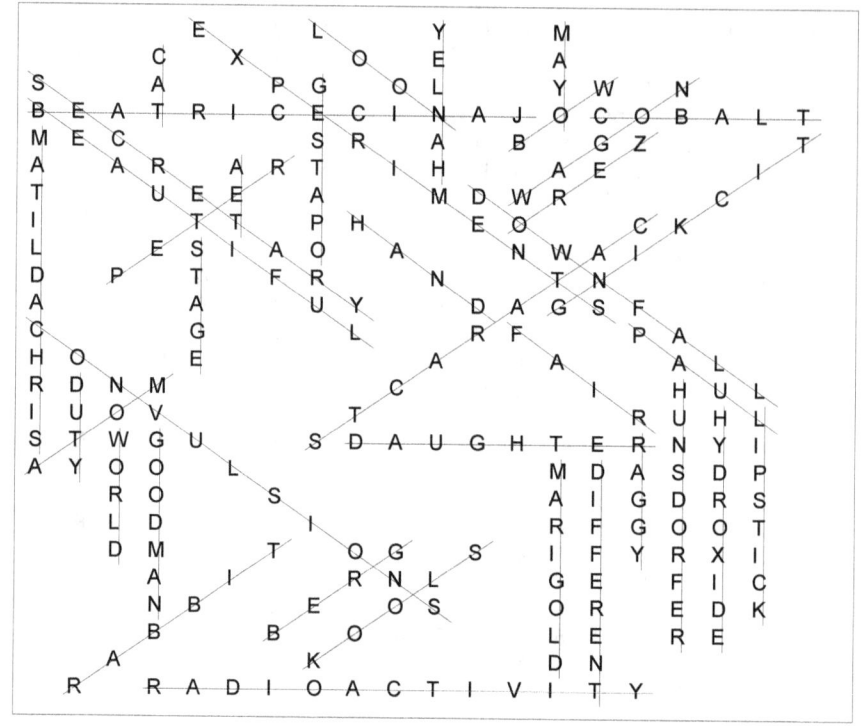

ATOM	EXPERIMENTS	MAYO
BEATRICE	FAIR	PAUL
BEAUTIFUL	GESTAPO	PETER
BERG	GOODMAN	RABBIT
BOW	HAND	RADIOACTIVITY
CAT	HANLEY	RAGGY
CATARACTS	HUNSDORFER	SECRETARY
CHRIS	HYDROXIDE	STAGE
COBALT	JANICE	TEA
CONVULSIONS	KOOLS	TICKING
DAUGHTER	LIPSTICK	WAGON
DIFFERENT	LOON	WORLD
DOWNFALL	MARIGOLD	ZERO
DUTY	MATILDA	

Effect of Gamma Rays Crossword 1

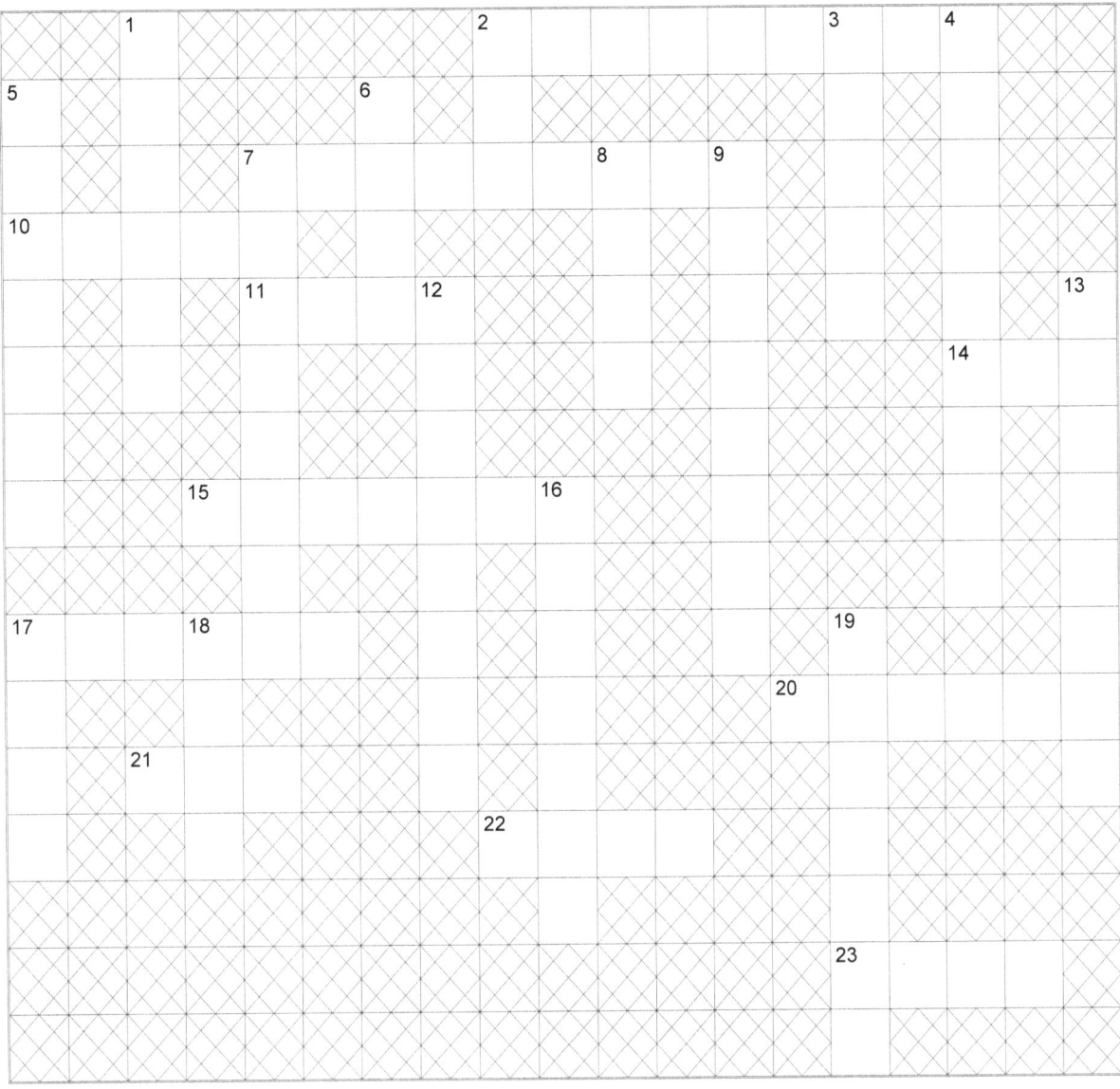

Across
2. Nanny has what in her eyes?
7. Tillie tells her mother, "Mama, you look ___!"
10. Beatrice is invited to sit there with mothers of the other finalists
11. Small thing that existed since the beginning of the world
14. Kind of shop Beatrice wants to open
15. Nanny's movements are like a ____ clock.
17. Gym teacher
20. Girl who did the cat project: ____ Vickery
21. Ruth says Tillie's hair ___ will make people laugh
22. Author: ____ Zindel
23. Going to the bathroom is Nanny's ____.

Down
1. Marigold seeds were exposed to ___-60
2. Janice Vickery boiled one in a pot
3. Ruth is worried about being embarrassed in front of ___ Burns.
4. Ruth is Mr. Goodman's ____.
5. German security police during Nazi regime
6. Ruth has nightmares about Mr. ____.
7. The mother in the book
8. Ruth tells Beatrice that Tillie is one of the finalists in the science ___
9. Ruth and Beatrice share ___ and cigarettes.
12. Tillie is raising ____ seeds.
13. Nanny was left with Beatrice by her ____.
16. Science teacher
17. Part of Tillie's body that came from a star
18. In high school Beatrice was called Betty the ____.
19. Tillie's real name

Effect of Gamma Rays Crossword 1 Answer Key

		1 C			2 C	A	T	A	R	3 A	C	T	4 S	
5 G		O		6 M	A					H			E	
E		B	7 B	E	A	U	T	8 I	9 F	U	L		R		C
10 S	T	A	G	E		Y			A	I		I		R	
T		L		11 A	T	O	12 M		I		P		S		E	13 D
A		T		T			A		R		S			14 T	E	A
P				R			R				T			A		U
O		15 T	I	C	K	I	N	16 G		I				R		G
				C			G		O		C			Y		H
17 H	18 A	N	L	E	Y		O		O		K		19 M			T
A		N					L		D			20 J	A	N	I	C	E
N		21 B	O	W			D		M				T			R
D		O				22 P	A	U	L				I			
		N							N				L			
												23 D	U	T	Y	
													A			

Across

2. Nanny has what in her eyes?
7. Tillie tells her mother, "Mama, you look ___!"
10. Beatrice is invited to sit there with mothers of the other finalists
11. Small thing that existed since the beginning of the world
14. Kind of shop Beatrice wants to open
15. Nanny's movements are like a ____ clock.
17. Gym teacher
20. Girl who did the cat project: ____ Vickery
21. Ruth says Tillie's hair ___ will make people laugh
22. Author: ____ Zindel
23. Going to the bathroom is Nanny's ____.

Down

1. Marigold seeds were exposed to ___-60
2. Janice Vickery boiled one in a pot
3. Ruth is worried about being embarrassed in front of ____ Burns.
4. Ruth is Mr. Goodman's ____.
5. German security police during Nazi regime
6. Ruth has nightmares about Mr. ____.
7. The mother in the book
8. Ruth tells Beatrice that Tillie is one of the finalists in the science ___
9. Ruth and Beatrice share ___ and cigarettes.
12. Tillie is raising ____ seeds.
13. Nanny was left with Beatrice by her ____.
16. Science teacher
17. Part of Tillie's body that came from a star
18. In high school Beatrice was called Betty the ____.
19. Tillie's real name

Effect of Gamma Rays Crossword 2

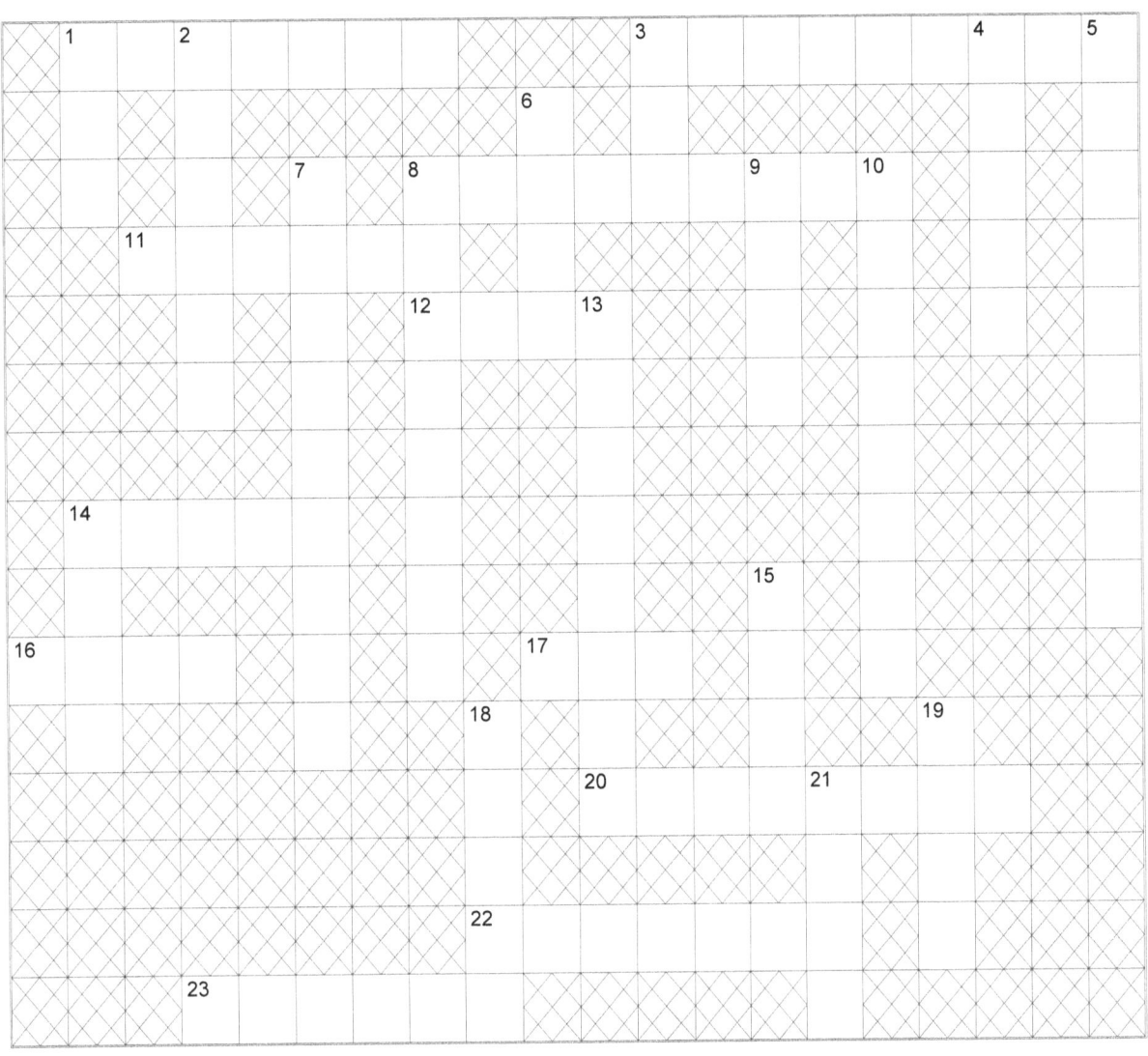

Across
1. Nanny's movements are like a ____ clock.
3. Nanny has what in her eyes?
8. Tillie tells her mother, "Mama, you look __!"
11. Girl who did the cat project: ____ Vickery
12. Small thing that existed since the beginning of the world
14. Rabbit's name
16. Going to the bathroom is Nanny's ____.
17. Ruth says Tillie's hair ___ will make people laugh
20. Nanny was left with Beatrice by her ____.
22. Science teacher
23. Gym teacher

Down
1. Kind of shop Beatrice wants to open
2. Marigold seeds were exposed to ___-60
3. Janice Vickery boiled one in a pot
4. Ruth is worried about being embarrassed in front of ___ Burns.
5. Ruth is Mr. Goodman's ____.
6. Ruth has nightmares about Mr. ____.
7. Beatrice says the world kills off people who are ____.
8. The mother in the book
9. Ruth tells Beatrice that Tillie is one of the finalists in the science ___
10. Ruth and Beatrice share ___ and cigarettes.
13. Tillie is raising ____ seeds.
14. Author: ____ Zindel
15. Principal's name: Dr. ____.
18. What Tillie's slip was
19. When Beatrice took stock of her life, she came up with ___
21. Part of Tillie's body that came from a star

Effect of Gamma Rays Crossword 2 Answer Key

	1 T	2 I	C	K	I	N	G		3 C	A	T	A	R	A	4 C	5 S
	E		O					6 M		A					H	E
	A		B		7 D		8 B	E	A	U	T	I	9 F	10 U	L	R	C
		11 J	A	N	I	C	E		Y				A		I		R
			L		F		12 A	T	13 O	M			I		P	S	E
			T		F		T		M				R		S		T
					E		R		A				T				A
		14 P	E	T	E	R		I		I					I		R
		A			E		C		G			15 B		C		Y
16 D	U	T	Y		N		E		17 B	O	W		E		K		
		L					T		18 R		L		R			19 Z	
									A		20 D	A	U	G	21 H	T	E	R
									G						A		R	
									22 G	O	O	D	M	A	N		O	
			23 H	A	N	L	E	Y							D			

Across
1. Nanny's movements are like a ____ clock.
3. Nanny has what in her eyes?
8. Tillie tells her mother, "Mama, you look __!"
11. Girl who did the cat project: ____ Vickery
12. Small thing that existed since the beginning of the world
14. Rabbit's name
16. Going to the bathroom is Nanny's ____.
17. Ruth says Tillie's hair ___ will make people laugh
20. Nanny was left with Beatrice by her ____.
22. Science teacher
23. Gym teacher

Down
1. Kind of shop Beatrice wants to open
2. Marigold seeds were exposed to ___-60
3. Janice Vickery boiled one in a pot
4. Ruth is worried about being embarrassed in front of ___ Burns.
5. Ruth is Mr. Goodman's ____.
6. Ruth has nightmares about Mr. ____.
7. Beatrice says the world kills off people who are ____.
8. The mother in the book
9. Ruth tells Beatrice that Tillie is one of the finalists in the science ___
10. Ruth and Beatrice share ___ and cigarettes.
13. Tillie is raising ____ seeds.
14. Author: ____ Zindel
15. Principal's name: Dr. ____.
18. What Tillie's slip was
19. When Beatrice took stock of her life, she came up with ___
21. Part of Tillie's body that came from a star

Effect of Gamma Rays Crossword 3

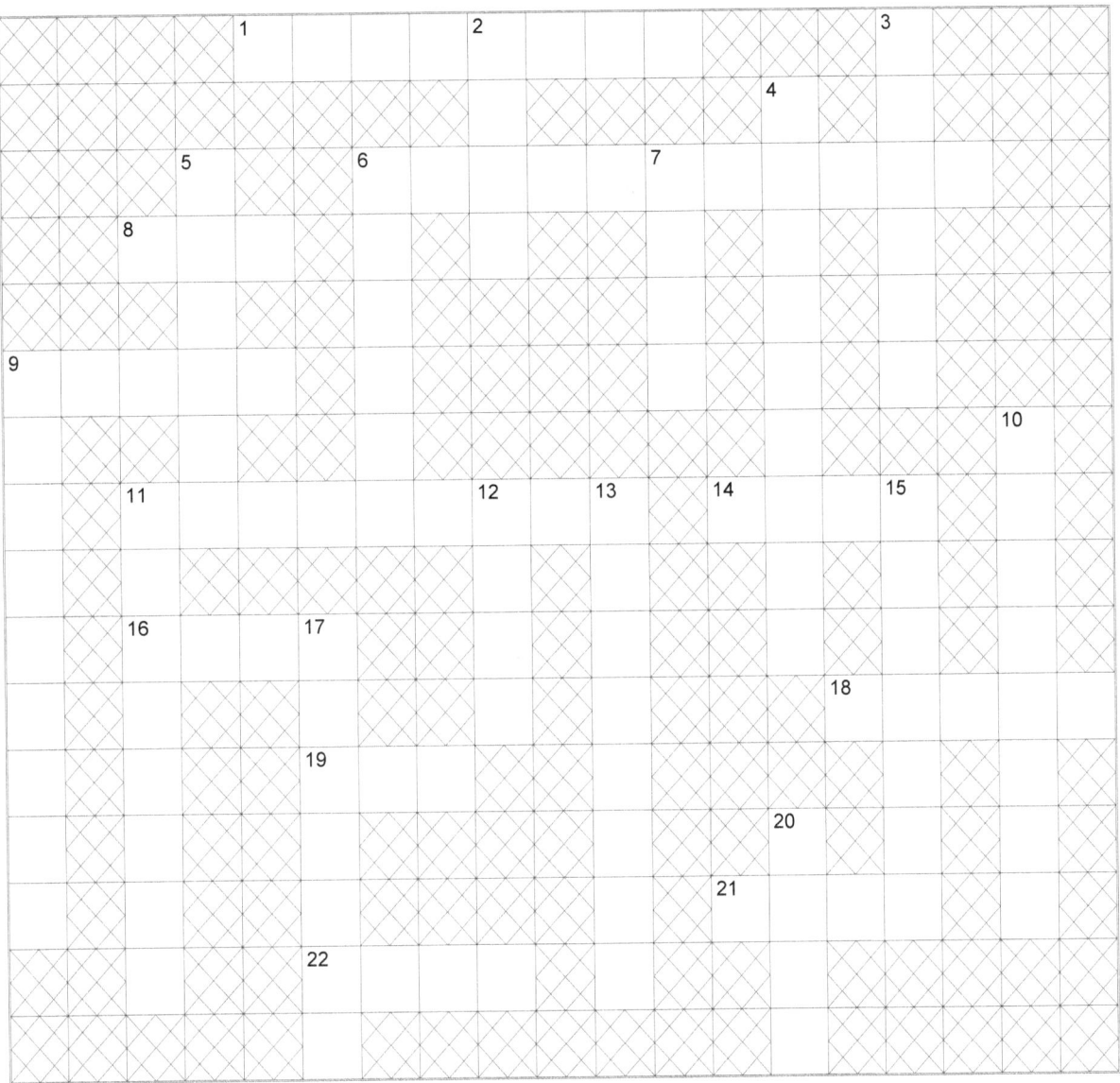

Across
1. Nanny was left with Beatrice by her ____.
6. Ruth's biggest problem is that she has ____.
8. Janice Vickery boiled one in a pot
9. Ruth is worried about being embarrassed in front of ___ Burns.
11. Tillie tells her mother, "Mama, you look __!"
14. Principal's name: Dr. ____.
16. Small thing that existed since the beginning of the world
18. Beatrice is invited to sit there with mothers of the other finalists
19. Kind of shop Beatrice wants to open
21. Ruth has nightmares about Mr. ____.
22. Going to the bathroom is Nanny's ____.

Down
2. Part of Tillie's body that came from a star
3. Gym teacher
4. Beatrice says the world kills off people who are ____.
5. Girl who did the cat project: ____ Vickery
6. Marigold seeds were exposed to ___-60
7. In high school Beatrice was called Betty the ____.
9. Nanny has what in her eyes?
10. Tillie is raising ____ seeds.
11. The mother in the book
12. Ruth tells Beatrice that Tillie is one of the finalists in the science ___
13. Ruth and Beatrice share ___ and cigarettes.
15. German security police during Nazi regime
17. Tillie's real name
20. Author: ____ Zindel

Effect of Gamma Rays Crossword 3 Answer Key

				1 D	A	U	2 G H A	T	E	R		3 H A	
											4 D	A	
			5 J		6 C	O	N	V	7 U L	S	I	O	N S
		8 C	A	T	O		D		O		F	L	
			N		B				O		F	E	
9 C	H	R	I	S	A				N		E	Y	
A			C		L				R				10 M
T		11 B	E	A	U	T	12 I	13 F	U	L	14 B	15 G	A
A		E					F	A	I		E	E	R
R		16 A	T	O	17 M		I		P		N	S	I
A		T			A		R		S		T	18 S T A G E
C		R			19 T	E	A		T			A	O
T		I			I				I		20 P	A	L
S		C			L				C	21 M	A	Y	O D
		E			22 D	U	T	Y	K	U			L
					A					L			

Across
1. Nanny was left with Beatrice by her ____.
6. Ruth's biggest problem is that she has ____.
8. Janice Vickery boiled one in a pot
9. Ruth is worried about being embarrassed in front of ___ Burns.
11. Tillie tells her mother, "Mama, you look __!"
14. Principal's name: Dr. ____.
16. Small thing that existed since the beginning of the world
18. Beatrice is invited to sit there with mothers of the other finalists
19. Kind of shop Beatrice wants to open
21. Ruth has nightmares about Mr. ____.
22. Going to the bathroom is Nanny's ____.

Down
2. Part of Tillie's body that came from a star
3. Gym teacher
4. Beatrice says the world kills off people who are ____.
5. Girl who did the cat project: ____ Vickery
6. Marigold seeds were exposed to ___-60
7. In high school Beatrice was called Betty the ____.
9. Nanny has what in her eyes?
10. Tillie is raising ____ seeds.
11. The mother in the book
12. Ruth tells Beatrice that Tillie is one of the finalists in the science ___
13. Ruth and Beatrice share ___ and cigarettes.
15. German security police during Nazi regime
17. Tillie's real name
20. Author: ____ Zindel

Effect of Gamma Rays Crossword 4

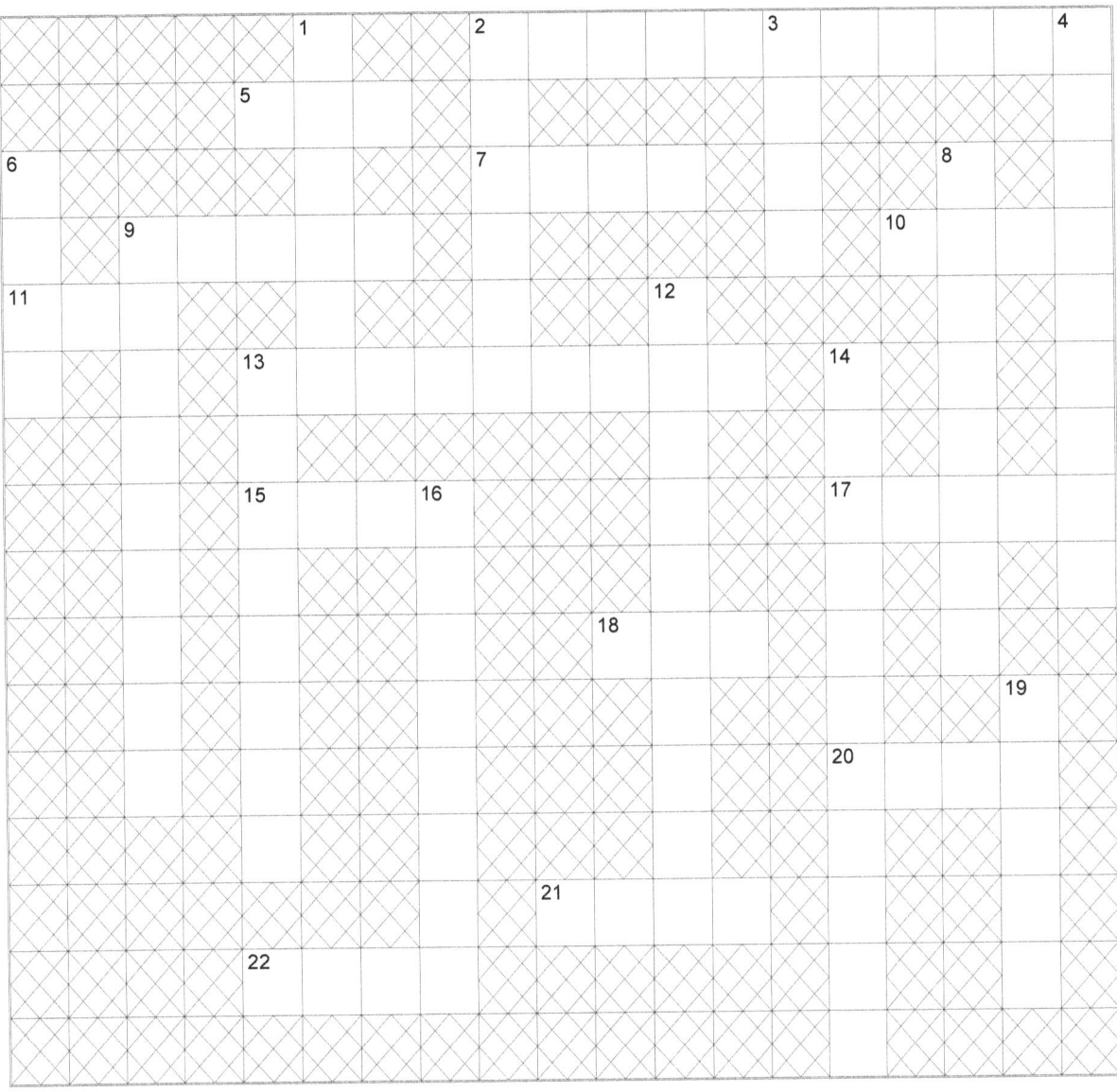

Across
2. Ruth's biggest problem is that she has ____.
5. Janice Vickery boiled one in a pot
7. Principal's name: Dr. ____.
9. Ruth is worried about being embarrassed in front of ___ Burns.
10. Ruth tells Beatrice that Tillie is one of the finalists in the science ___
11. Kind of shop Beatrice wants to open
13. Tillie tells her mother, "Mama, you look __!"
15. Small thing that existed since the beginning of the world
17. Rabbit's name
18. Ruth says Tillie's hair ___ will make people laugh
20. Ruth has nightmares about Mr. ____.
21. When Beatrice took stock of her life, she came up with ___
22. Part of Tillie's body that came from a star

Down
1. Girl who did the cat project: ____ Vickery
2. Marigold seeds were exposed to ___-60
3. In high school Beatrice was called Betty the ____.
4. Ruth is Mr. Goodman's ____.
6. Going to the bathroom is Nanny's ____.
8. Nanny was left with Beatrice by her ____.
9. Nanny has what in her eyes?
12. Beatrice's last name
13. The mother in the book
14. Tillie likes to do them
16. Tillie is raising ____ seeds.
19. Ruth's favorite cigarettes are ____.

Effect of Gamma Rays Crossword 4 Answer Key

				¹J		²C	O	N	V	³L	U	S	I	O	N	S	⁴S
			⁵C	A	T	O				O							E
⁶D				N		⁷B	E	R	G	O				⁸D			C
U		⁹C	H	R	I	S	A			N			¹⁰F	A	I	R
¹¹T	E	A			C		L		¹²H				U			E
Y		¹³T		B	E	A	U	T	I	F	U	L	¹⁴E		G	H	T	A
		A		E				N				X		H		A
		R		¹⁵A	T	O	¹⁶M			S		¹⁷P	E	T	E	R
		A		T			A			D		E		E		Y
		C		R			A		¹⁸B	O	W	R		R		
		T		I			I			R		I			¹⁹K	
		S		C			G			F		²⁰M	A	Y	O	
				E			O			E		E			O	
							²¹Z	E	R	O		N			L	
				²²H	A	N	D					T			S	
												S				

Across
2. Ruth's biggest problem is that she has ____.
5. Janice Vickery boiled one in a pot
7. Principal's name: Dr. ____.
9. Ruth is worried about being embarrassed in front of ____ Burns.
10. Ruth tells Beatrice that Tillie is one of the finalists in the science ___
11. Kind of shop Beatrice wants to open
13. Tillie tells her mother, "Mama, you look __!"
15. Small thing that existed since the beginning of the world
17. Rabbit's name
18. Ruth says Tillie's hair ___ will make people laugh
20. Ruth has nightmares about Mr. ____.
21. When Beatrice took stock of her life, she came up with ___
22. Part of Tillie's body that came from a star

Down
1. Girl who did the cat project: ____ Vickery
2. Marigold seeds were exposed to ___-60
3. In high school Beatrice was called Betty the ____.
4. Ruth is Mr. Goodman's ____.
6. Going to the bathroom is Nanny's ____.
8. Nanny was left with Beatrice by her ____.
9. Nanny has what in her eyes?
12. Beatrice's last name
13. The mother in the book
14. Tillie likes to do them
16. Tillie is raising ____ seeds.
19. Ruth's favorite cigarettes are ____.

Effect of Gamma Rays

PAUL	DOWNFALL	EXPERIMENTS	DAUGHTER	CAT
RAGGY	DIFFERENT	HYDROXIDE	BEATRICE	PETER
BERG	GOODMAN	FREE SPACE	COBALT	MATILDA
TEA	MAYO	HAND	HUNSDORFER	TICKING
CHRIS	STAGE	ZERO	KOOLS	ATOM

Effect of Gamma Rays

CATARACTS	FAIR	RADIOACTIVITY	CONVULSIONS	BOW
MARIGOLD	LIPSTICK	WORLD	SECRETARY	GESTAPO
WAGON	BEAUTIFUL	FREE SPACE	JANICE	RABBIT
DUTY	ATOM	KOOLS	ZERO	STAGE
CHRIS	TICKING	HUNSDORFER	HAND	MAYO

Effect of Gamma Rays

LIPSTICK	MATILDA	ZERO	HUNSDORFER	DIFFERENT
DUTY	HANLEY	TICKING	GESTAPO	LOON
BEAUTIFUL	RADIOACTIVITY	FREE SPACE	SECRETARY	GOODMAN
KOOLS	CAT	HAND	EXPERIMENTS	JANICE
ATOM	COBALT	TEA	PAUL	RABBIT

Effect of Gamma Rays

WAGON	DOWNFALL	FAIR	BOW	PETER
WORLD	DAUGHTER	STAGE	HYDROXIDE	MARIGOLD
CHRIS	CONVULSIONS	FREE SPACE	BERG	CATARACTS
RAGGY	RABBIT	PAUL	TEA	COBALT
ATOM	JANICE	EXPERIMENTS	HAND	CAT

Effect of Gamma Rays

GESTAPO	HUNSDORFER	PETER	HAND	CHRIS
RABBIT	LIPSTICK	CATARACTS	TICKING	ATOM
BEAUTIFUL	SECRETARY	FREE SPACE	KOOLS	RADIOACTIVITY
CAT	COBALT	DAUGHTER	CONVULSIONS	RAGGY
DUTY	FAIR	ZERO	WORLD	WAGON

Effect of Gamma Rays

LOON	DIFFERENT	PAUL	GOODMAN	EXPERIMENTS
MARIGOLD	STAGE	BOW	DOWNFALL	BEATRICE
JANICE	TEA	FREE SPACE	MAYO	BERG
HYDROXIDE	WAGON	WORLD	ZERO	FAIR
DUTY	RAGGY	CONVULSIONS	DAUGHTER	COBALT

Effect of Gamma Rays

CATARACTS	RABBIT	MAYO	WORLD	DAUGHTER
BERG	HANLEY	FAIR	ATOM	GOODMAN
HUNSDORFER	DUTY	FREE SPACE	BEAUTIFUL	CAT
LOON	LIPSTICK	SECRETARY	WAGON	DOWNFALL
ZERO	MATILDA	TICKING	CONVULSIONS	HYDROXIDE

Effect of Gamma Rays

BEATRICE	RADIOACTIVITY	COBALT	GESTAPO	KOOLS
DIFFERENT	JANICE	RAGGY	EXPERIMENTS	PETER
STAGE	BOW	FREE SPACE	HAND	TEA
CHRIS	HYDROXIDE	CONVULSIONS	TICKING	MATILDA
ZERO	DOWNFALL	WAGON	SECRETARY	LIPSTICK

Copyrighted

Effect of Gamma Rays

LOON	TEA	DUTY	WORLD	BOW
TICKING	DOWNFALL	PETER	CONVULSIONS	PAUL
EXPERIMENTS	MATILDA	FREE SPACE	GOODMAN	KOOLS
ZERO	BEATRICE	HYDROXIDE	LIPSTICK	SECRETARY
HAND	RABBIT	CAT	JANICE	HUNSDORFER

Effect of Gamma Rays

BERG	STAGE	DAUGHTER	MARIGOLD	WAGON
FAIR	GESTAPO	CATARACTS	HANLEY	BEAUTIFUL
ATOM	RAGGY	FREE SPACE	MAYO	RADIOACTIVITY
DIFFERENT	HUNSDORFER	JANICE	CAT	RABBIT
HAND	SECRETARY	LIPSTICK	HYDROXIDE	BEATRICE

Effect of Gamma Rays

ATOM	ZERO	RADIOACTIVITY	COBALT	PETER
DUTY	HAND	RABBIT	LOON	DAUGHTER
WORLD	CAT	FREE SPACE	HYDROXIDE	TICKING
DOWNFALL	WAGON	STAGE	GESTAPO	HUNSDORFER
KOOLS	MAYO	DIFFERENT	GOODMAN	EXPERIMENTS

Effect of Gamma Rays

FAIR	CONVULSIONS	CHRIS	JANICE	CATARACTS
BEAUTIFUL	BERG	LIPSTICK	BEATRICE	PAUL
RAGGY	BOW	FREE SPACE	SECRETARY	TEA
MARIGOLD	EXPERIMENTS	GOODMAN	DIFFERENT	MAYO
KOOLS	HUNSDORFER	GESTAPO	STAGE	WAGON

Effect of Gamma Rays

GOODMAN	BOW	KOOLS	TICKING	RABBIT
EXPERIMENTS	PETER	SECRETARY	BEATRICE	DUTY
MATILDA	BERG	FREE SPACE	MAYO	WAGON
CATARACTS	HAND	TEA	ATOM	STAGE
JANICE	DAUGHTER	CAT	COBALT	HANLEY

Effect of Gamma Rays

LOON	RADIOACTIVITY	CONVULSIONS	GESTAPO	DOWNFALL
FAIR	ZERO	LIPSTICK	DIFFERENT	RAGGY
WORLD	PAUL	FREE SPACE	HUNSDORFER	MARIGOLD
HYDROXIDE	HANLEY	COBALT	CAT	DAUGHTER
JANICE	STAGE	ATOM	TEA	HAND

Effect of Gamma Rays

TICKING	WORLD	PAUL	HANLEY	BEATRICE
MATILDA	EXPERIMENTS	CATARACTS	DAUGHTER	BEAUTIFUL
COBALT	HAND	FREE SPACE	SECRETARY	CAT
DIFFERENT	HUNSDORFER	CHRIS	FAIR	CONVULSIONS
GESTAPO	LIPSTICK	DUTY	BERG	WAGON

Effect of Gamma Rays

JANICE	ATOM	RABBIT	GOODMAN	MAYO
RAGGY	LOON	STAGE	TEA	RADIOACTIVITY
KOOLS	HYDROXIDE	FREE SPACE	BOW	MARIGOLD
ZERO	WAGON	BERG	DUTY	LIPSTICK
GESTAPO	CONVULSIONS	FAIR	CHRIS	HUNSDORFER

Effect of Gamma Rays

GOODMAN	DOWNFALL	RAGGY	KOOLS	BEATRICE
RABBIT	PETER	CHRIS	HYDROXIDE	ZERO
LIPSTICK	MAYO	FREE SPACE	FAIR	MARIGOLD
MATILDA	TEA	WAGON	HAND	BOW
ATOM	WORLD	RADIOACTIVITY	BEAUTIFUL	STAGE

Effect of Gamma Rays

GESTAPO	PAUL	CAT	JANICE	COBALT
SECRETARY	DAUGHTER	TICKING	LOON	HUNSDORFER
CONVULSIONS	BERG	FREE SPACE	EXPERIMENTS	DIFFERENT
HANLEY	STAGE	BEAUTIFUL	RADIOACTIVITY	WORLD
ATOM	BOW	HAND	WAGON	TEA

Effect of Gamma Rays

WORLD	FAIR	HUNSDORFER	CHRIS	TEA
HYDROXIDE	DUTY	ATOM	RADIOACTIVITY	MARIGOLD
PETER	CAT	FREE SPACE	STAGE	MAYO
PAUL	GOODMAN	LOON	BEATRICE	JANICE
HANLEY	CATARACTS	WAGON	ZERO	BERG

Effect of Gamma Rays

BEAUTIFUL	TICKING	SECRETARY	LIPSTICK	CONVULSIONS
KOOLS	DAUGHTER	GESTAPO	MATILDA	HAND
DIFFERENT	RABBIT	FREE SPACE	DOWNFALL	RAGGY
BOW	BERG	ZERO	WAGON	CATARACTS
HANLEY	JANICE	BEATRICE	LOON	GOODMAN

Effect of Gamma Rays

HUNSDORFER	JANICE	MARIGOLD	GESTAPO	GOODMAN
MAYO	ZERO	RAGGY	COBALT	SECRETARY
PETER	CONVULSIONS	FREE SPACE	EXPERIMENTS	BOW
HYDROXIDE	FAIR	TICKING	CAT	CATARACTS
WORLD	KOOLS	RABBIT	RADIOACTIVITY	BERG

Effect of Gamma Rays

BEATRICE	HANLEY	MATILDA	DOWNFALL	HAND
LOON	PAUL	BEAUTIFUL	ATOM	DAUGHTER
LIPSTICK	WAGON	FREE SPACE	STAGE	CHRIS
DIFFERENT	BERG	RADIOACTIVITY	RABBIT	KOOLS
WORLD	CATARACTS	CAT	TICKING	FAIR

Effect of Gamma Rays

DUTY	SECRETARY	PAUL	BERG	RABBIT
LIPSTICK	ZERO	BEAUTIFUL	RAGGY	CATARACTS
RADIOACTIVITY	HUNSDORFER	FREE SPACE	BEATRICE	WORLD
DAUGHTER	GESTAPO	HANLEY	TEA	TICKING
MARIGOLD	LOON	JANICE	PETER	ATOM

Effect of Gamma Rays

WAGON	CAT	MAYO	STAGE	KOOLS
COBALT	GOODMAN	DIFFERENT	CHRIS	BOW
EXPERIMENTS	DOWNFALL	FREE SPACE	FAIR	MATILDA
HAND	ATOM	PETER	JANICE	LOON
MARIGOLD	TICKING	TEA	HANLEY	GESTAPO

Effect of Gamma Rays

CONVULSIONS	KOOLS	DAUGHTER	SECRETARY	MAYO
LOON	TICKING	CATARACTS	HANLEY	PAUL
RABBIT	BERG	FREE SPACE	DOWNFALL	LIPSTICK
TEA	BOW	RADIOACTIVITY	DUTY	CAT
ATOM	STAGE	WAGON	BEATRICE	PETER

Effect of Gamma Rays

HUNSDORFER	JANICE	GOODMAN	ZERO	HYDROXIDE
DIFFERENT	RAGGY	EXPERIMENTS	HAND	BEAUTIFUL
MARIGOLD	MATILDA	FREE SPACE	COBALT	WORLD
GESTAPO	PETER	BEATRICE	WAGON	STAGE
ATOM	CAT	DUTY	RADIOACTIVITY	BOW

Effect of Gamma Rays

SECRETARY	MAYO	FAIR	ZERO	WORLD
WAGON	HAND	TICKING	BOW	GOODMAN
RAGGY	MARIGOLD	FREE SPACE	GESTAPO	KOOLS
DIFFERENT	STAGE	RADIOACTIVITY	CHRIS	RABBIT
CATARACTS	CAT	TEA	DUTY	LIPSTICK

Effect of Gamma Rays

BEATRICE	DOWNFALL	COBALT	HYDROXIDE	LOON
CONVULSIONS	PAUL	HANLEY	BERG	DAUGHTER
HUNSDORFER	EXPERIMENTS	FREE SPACE	JANICE	ATOM
MATILDA	LIPSTICK	DUTY	TEA	CAT
CATARACTS	RABBIT	CHRIS	RADIOACTIVITY	STAGE

Effect of Gamma Rays

GESTAPO	BEATRICE	HUNSDORFER	PETER	PAUL
BERG	WORLD	BEAUTIFUL	DAUGHTER	LOON
JANICE	STAGE	FREE SPACE	FAIR	SECRETARY
LIPSTICK	HYDROXIDE	TICKING	ATOM	TEA
CONVULSIONS	GOODMAN	KOOLS	HANLEY	EXPERIMENTS

Effect of Gamma Rays

RADIOACTIVITY	DOWNFALL	COBALT	RABBIT	CHRIS
RAGGY	ZERO	DIFFERENT	WAGON	BOW
CAT	HAND	FREE SPACE	MAYO	CATARACTS
MARIGOLD	EXPERIMENTS	HANLEY	KOOLS	GOODMAN
CONVULSIONS	TEA	ATOM	TICKING	HYDROXIDE

Effect of Gamma Rays

WORLD	JANICE	CHRIS	CONVULSIONS	TICKING
STAGE	PAUL	ZERO	DUTY	SECRETARY
PETER	MAYO	FREE SPACE	COBALT	GESTAPO
CAT	TEA	HANLEY	RABBIT	ATOM
DIFFERENT	FAIR	BERG	DAUGHTER	LOON

Effect of Gamma Rays

RAGGY	BEAUTIFUL	MARIGOLD	BOW	MATILDA
EXPERIMENTS	HYDROXIDE	KOOLS	WAGON	GOODMAN
HAND	BEATRICE	FREE SPACE	CATARACTS	RADIOACTIVITY
LIPSTICK	LOON	DAUGHTER	BERG	FAIR
DIFFERENT	ATOM	RABBIT	HANLEY	TEA

Gamma Rays Vocabulary Word List

No.	Word	Clue/Definition
1.	ACCENTUATED	Stressed; accented
2.	ANATOMY	Structure of an organism or organ
3.	ANCIENT	Very old
4.	ATOM	Smallest unit of an element
5.	BERSERK	Deranged; crazed
6.	BOGEYMAN	A terrifying presence; hobgoblin
7.	CALCULATES	Computes mathematically
8.	CATARACTS	Opacities of the eye lens or capsule
9.	CHLOROFORM	Chemical to anesthetize or kill
10.	COMMENCES	Starts
11.	COMPETITION	Others capable of winning
12.	CONVULSIONS	Intense involuntary muscular contractions
13.	COOT	An eccentric person
14.	EAVESDROPPING	Listening secretly
15.	ECSTASY	Intense joy or delight
16.	EFFEMINATE	Having qualities usually associated with females
17.	ETERNITY	Continuance without beginning or end
18.	EXAGGERATING	Enlarging, increasing beyond normal bounds
19.	EXASPERATE	Make angry or impatient
20.	FERMENT	To seethe; to be agitated
21.	FLINGING	Casting aside; discarding
22.	GASPS	Sharp breaths
23.	HALFLIFE	Time for half of nuclei to radioactively decay
24.	HORRIFIES	Scares; shocks; causes horror
25.	HYSTERICAL	Having excessive or uncontrollable emotion
26.	INCONSPICUOUS	Not readily noticeable
27.	JEALOUS	Envious
28.	LOON	One who is crazy or simple-minded
29.	MECHANICALLY	Like a machine
30.	MIMEOGRAPHED	Copies
31.	MISBEGOTTEN	Of dubious origins
32.	MUTATION	A change, as in nature, form, or quality
33.	NERVE	Brazen boldness
34.	OBLIVIOUS	Unaware of
35.	PATHETIC	Arousing sympathy and compassion
36.	PECULIAR	Odd
37.	PERVADES	Spreads throughout
38.	PRIMEVAL	Belonging to the first or earliest age or ages
39.	PSORIASIS	A skin disease
40.	PUNCTUATES	Emphasizes
41.	RADIOACTIVITY	Spontaneous emission of radiation
42.	RUMMAGES	Makes a disorderly search of
43.	RUSTLING	Soft fluttering or crackling sounds
44.	SACCHARINE	Sweet
45.	SANATORIUM	A place of convalescence from illness
46.	SHUFFLING	Sliding feet along the floor
47.	SILHOUETTE	Outline or profile
48.	SINISTER	Threatening evil
49.	SMUG	Self-satisfied; complacent
50.	SNOOP	One who pries secretly
51.	STAGGERING	Overwhelming

Gamma Rays Vocabulary Word List Continued

No.	Word	Clue/Definition
52.	STERILITY	Incapability of producing offspring
53.	SUFFOCATE	Kill by preventing access to oxygen
54.	SURVEYS	Examines; looks at comprehensively
55.	THROMBOSIS	Blood clot in blood vessel or heart
56.	TRANSPLANT	Uproot and replant
57.	TREMBLE	Shake violently
58.	TRIGGERS	Precipitates; causes to happen
59.	VIBRATES	Shakes or trembles
60.	VICIOUS	Savage; evil; dangerous

Gamma Rays Vocabulary Fill In The Blank 1

_____ 1. Kill by preventing access to oxygen

_____ 2. Examines; looks at comprehensively

_____ 3. A skin disease

_____ 4. Of dubious origins

_____ 5. Having qualities usually associated with females

_____ 6. Spreads throughout

_____ 7. Belonging to the first or earliest age or ages

_____ 8. One who pries secretly

_____ 9. Savage; evil; dangerous

_____ 10. Intense joy or delight

_____ 11. Intense involuntary muscular contractions

_____ 12. Sharp breaths

_____ 13. Enlarging, increasing beyond normal bounds

_____ 14. One who is crazy or simple-minded

_____ 15. Soft fluttering or crackling sounds

_____ 16. Opacities of the eye lens or capsule

_____ 17. Shakes or trembles

_____ 18. An eccentric person

_____ 19. Shake violently

_____ 20. Very old

Gamma Rays Vocabulary Fill In The Blank 1 Answer Key

SUFFOCATE	1. Kill by preventing access to oxygen
SURVEYS	2. Examines; looks at comprehensively
PSORIASIS	3. A skin disease
MISBEGOTTEN	4. Of dubious origins
EFFEMINATE	5. Having qualities usually associated with females
PERVADES	6. Spreads throughout
PRIMEVAL	7. Belonging to the first or earliest age or ages
SNOOP	8. One who pries secretly
VICIOUS	9. Savage; evil; dangerous
ECSTASY	10. Intense joy or delight
CONVULSIONS	11. Intense involuntary muscular contractions
GASPS	12. Sharp breaths
EXAGGERATING	13. Enlarging, increasing beyond normal bounds
LOON	14. One who is crazy or simple-minded
RUSTLING	15. Soft fluttering or crackling sounds
CATARACTS	16. Opacities of the eye lens or capsule
VIBRATES	17. Shakes or trembles
COOT	18. An eccentric person
TREMBLE	19. Shake violently
ANCIENT	20. Very old

Gamma Rays Vocabulary Fil In The Blank 2

1. One who pries secretly
2. Starts
3. Soft fluttering or crackling sounds
4. Scares; shocks; causes horror
5. Intense involuntary muscular contractions
6. Belonging to the first or earliest age or ages
7. Self-satisfied; complacent
8. Blood clot in blood vessel or heart
9. Like a machine
10. A place of convalescence from illness
11. Kill by preventing access to oxygen
12. Unaware of
13. Chemical to anesthetize or kill
14. Computes mathematically
15. Arousing sympathy and compassion
16. To seethe; to be agitated
17. Structure of an organism or organ
18. Savage; evil; dangerous
19. Opacities of the eye lens or capsule
20. Others capable of winning

Gamma Rays Vocabulary Fill In The Blank 2 Answer Key

SNOOP	1. One who pries secretly
COMMENCES	2. Starts
RUSTLING	3. Soft fluttering or crackling sounds
HORRIFIES	4. Scares; shocks; causes horror
CONVULSIONS	5. Intense involuntary muscular contractions
PRIMEVAL	6. Belonging to the first or earliest age or ages
SMUG	7. Self-satisfied; complacent
THROMBOSIS	8. Blood clot in blood vessel or heart
MECHANICALLY	9. Like a machine
SANATORIUM	10. A place of convalescence from illness
SUFFOCATE	11. Kill by preventing access to oxygen
OBLIVIOUS	12. Unaware of
CHLOROFORM	13. Chemical to anesthetize or kill
CALCULATES	14. Computes mathematically
PATHETIC	15. Arousing sympathy and compassion
FERMENT	16. To seethe; to be agitated
ANATOMY	17. Structure of an organism or organ
VICIOUS	18. Savage; evil; dangerous
CATARACTS	19. Opacities of the eye lens or capsule
COMPETITION	20. Others capable of winning

Gamma Rays Vocabulary Fill In The Blank 3

_____ 1. Kill by preventing access to oxygen

_____ 2. Uproot and replant

_____ 3. To seethe; to be agitated

_____ 4. Of dubious origins

_____ 5. Belonging to the first or earliest age or ages

_____ 6. Chemical to anesthetize or kill

_____ 7. Sweet

_____ 8. Not readily noticeable

_____ 9. Sliding feet along the floor

_____ 10. Makes a disorderly search of

_____ 11. Make angry or impatient

_____ 12. Savage; evil; dangerous

_____ 13. Others capable of winning

_____ 14. Spreads throughout

_____ 15. Starts

_____ 16. Copies

_____ 17. Threatening evil

_____ 18. Unaware of

_____ 19. Brazen boldness

_____ 20. Listening secretly

Gamma Rays Vocabulary Fill In The Blank 3 Answer Key

SUFFOCATE	1. Kill by preventing access to oxygen
TRANSPLANT	2. Uproot and replant
FERMENT	3. To seethe; to be agitated
MISBEGOTTEN	4. Of dubious origins
PRIMEVAL	5. Belonging to the first or earliest age or ages
CHLOROFORM	6. Chemical to anesthetize or kill
SACCHARINE	7. Sweet
INCONSPICUOUS	8. Not readily noticeable
SHUFFLING	9. Sliding feet along the floor
RUMMAGES	10. Makes a disorderly search of
EXASPERATE	11. Make angry or impatient
VICIOUS	12. Savage; evil; dangerous
COMPETITION	13. Others capable of winning
PERVADES	14. Spreads throughout
COMMENCES	15. Starts
MIMEOGRAPHED	16. Copies
SINISTER	17. Threatening evil
OBLIVIOUS	18. Unaware of
NERVE	19. Brazen boldness
EAVESDROPPING	20. Listening secretly

Gamma Rays Vocabulary Fill In The Blank 4

1. Of dubious origins
2. Uproot and replant
3. Listening secretly
4. Odd
5. Time for half of nuclei to radioactively decay
6. Spontaneous emission of radiation
7. Shake violently
8. Incapability of producing offspring
9. Starts
10. Self-satisfied; complacent
11. Outline or profile
12. Enlarging, increasing beyond normal bounds
13. A terrifying presence; hobgoblin
14. Intense involuntary muscular contractions
15. Examines; looks at comprehensively
16. Chemical to anesthetize or kill
17. Copies
18. Not readily noticeable
19. Having excessive or uncontrollable emotion
20. Continuance without beginning or end

Gamma Rays Vocabulary Fill In The Blank 4 Answer Key

MISBEGOTTEN		1. Of dubious origins
TRANSPLANT		2. Uproot and replant
EAVESDROPPING		3. Listening secretly
PECULIAR		4. Odd
HALFLIFE		5. Time for half of nuclei to radioactively decay
RADIOACTIVITY		6. Spontaneous emission of radiation
TREMBLE		7. Shake violently
STERILITY		8. Incapability of producing offspring
COMMENCES		9. Starts
SMUG		10. Self-satisfied; complacent
SILHOUETTE		11. Outline or profile
EXAGGERATING		12. Enlarging, increasing beyond normal bounds
BOGEYMAN		13. A terrifying presence; hobgoblin
CONVULSIONS		14. Intense involuntary muscular contractions
SURVEYS		15. Examines; looks at comprehensively
CHLOROFORM		16. Chemical to anesthetize or kill
MIMEOGRAPHED		17. Copies
INCONSPICUOUS		18. Not readily noticeable
HYSTERICAL		19. Having excessive or uncontrollable emotion
ETERNITY		20. Continuance without beginning or end

Gamma Rays Vocabulary Matching 1

___ 1. SILHOUETTE   A. Sliding feet along the floor
___ 2. BOGEYMAN   B. Structure of an organism or organ
___ 3. RUMMAGES   C. Incapability of producing offspring
___ 4. MECHANICALLY   D. Unaware of
___ 5. SHUFFLING   E. Time for half of nuclei to radioactively decay
___ 6. HALFLIFE   F. Of dubious origins
___ 7. ANATOMY   G. A terrifying presence; hobgoblin
___ 8. GASPS   H. Soft fluttering or crackling sounds
___ 9. CATARACTS   I. Not readily noticeable
___ 10. OBLIVIOUS   J. Overwhelming
___ 11. THROMBOSIS   K. Opacities of the eye lens or capsule
___ 12. BERSERK   L. Uproot and replant
___ 13. SACCHARINE   M. Sweet
___ 14. EXASPERATE   N. Copies
___ 15. TRIGGERS   O. Precipitates; causes to happen
___ 16. INCONSPICUOUS   P. Self-satisfied; complacent
___ 17. STAGGERING   Q. Sharp breaths
___ 18. SMUG   R. Having qualities usually associated with females
___ 19. STERILITY   S. Like a machine
___ 20. COOT   T. Makes a disorderly search of
___ 21. RUSTLING   U. Outline or profile
___ 22. MISBEGOTTEN   V. An eccentric person
___ 23. MIMEOGRAPHED   W. Blood clot in blood vessel or heart
___ 24. TRANSPLANT   X. Deranged; crazed
___ 25. EFFEMINATE   Y. Make angry or impatient

Gamma Rays Vocabulary Matching 1 Answer Key

U - 1. SILHOUETTE		A. Sliding feet along the floor
G - 2. BOGEYMAN		B. Structure of an organism or organ
T - 3. RUMMAGES		C. Incapability of producing offspring
S - 4. MECHANICALLY		D. Unaware of
A - 5. SHUFFLING		E. Time for half of nuclei to radioactively decay
E - 6. HALFLIFE		F. Of dubious origins
B - 7. ANATOMY		G. A terrifying presence; hobgoblin
Q - 8. GASPS		H. Soft fluttering or crackling sounds
K - 9. CATARACTS		I. Not readily noticeable
D - 10. OBLIVIOUS		J. Overwhelming
W - 11. THROMBOSIS		K. Opacities of the eye lens or capsule
X - 12. BERSERK		L. Uproot and replant
M - 13. SACCHARINE		M. Sweet
Y - 14. EXASPERATE		N. Copies
O - 15. TRIGGERS		O. Precipitates; causes to happen
I - 16. INCONSPICUOUS		P. Self-satisfied; complacent
J - 17. STAGGERING		Q. Sharp breaths
P - 18. SMUG		R. Having qualities usually associated with females
C - 19. STERILITY		S. Like a machine
V - 20. COOT		T. Makes a disorderly search of
H - 21. RUSTLING		U. Outline or profile
F - 22. MISBEGOTTEN		V. An eccentric person
N - 23. MIMEOGRAPHED		W. Blood clot in blood vessel or heart
L - 24. TRANSPLANT		X. Deranged; crazed
R - 25. EFFEMINATE		Y. Make angry or impatient

Gamma Rays Vocabulary Matching 2

___ 1. BOGEYMAN
___ 2. SMUG
___ 3. SHUFFLING
___ 4. BERSERK
___ 5. THROMBOSIS
___ 6. COMPETITION
___ 7. CATARACTS
___ 8. CALCULATES
___ 9. GASPS
___ 10. INCONSPICUOUS
___ 11. PRIMEVAL
___ 12. COOT
___ 13. SACCHARINE
___ 14. PUNCTUATES
___ 15. MISBEGOTTEN
___ 16. HYSTERICAL
___ 17. VIBRATES
___ 18. COMMENCES
___ 19. JEALOUS
___ 20. PECULIAR
___ 21. VICIOUS
___ 22. TRIGGERS
___ 23. RADIOACTIVITY
___ 24. ATOM
___ 25. MIMEOGRAPHED

A. Emphasizes
B. Smallest unit of an element
C. Opacities of the eye lens or capsule
D. Starts
E. Precipitates; causes to happen
F. Spontaneous emission of radiation
G. Having excessive or uncontrollable emotion
H. An eccentric person
I. Others capable of winning
J. Envious
K. Blood clot in blood vessel or heart
L. Sharp breaths
M. computes mathematically
N. Deranged; crazed
O. Belonging to the first or earliest age or ages
P. Self-satisfied; complacent
Q. Not readily noticeable
R. A terrifying presence; hobgoblin
S. Of dubious origins
T. Sliding feet along the floor
U. Copies
V. Shakes or trembles
W. Savage; evil; dangerous
X. Sweet
Y. Odd

Gamma Rays Vocabulary Matching 2 Answer Key

R - 1. BOGEYMAN		A. Emphasizes
P - 2. SMUG		B. Smallest unit of an element
T - 3. SHUFFLING		C. Opacities of the eye lens or capsule
N - 4. BERSERK		D. Starts
K - 5. THROMBOSIS		E. Precipitates; causes to happen
I - 6. COMPETITION		F. Spontaneous emission of radiation
C - 7. CATARACTS		G. Having excessive or uncontrollable emotion
M - 8. CALCULATES		H. An eccentric person
L - 9. GASPS		I. Others capable of winning
Q - 10. INCONSPICUOUS		J. Envious
O - 11. PRIMEVAL		K. Blood clot in blood vessel or heart
H - 12. COOT		L. Sharp breaths
X - 13. SACCHARINE		M. computes mathematically
A - 14. PUNCTUATES		N. Deranged; crazed
S - 15. MISBEGOTTEN		O. Belonging to the first or earliest age or ages
G - 16. HYSTERICAL		P. Self-satisfied; complacent
V - 17. VIBRATES		Q. Not readily noticeable
D - 18. COMMENCES		R. A terrifying presence; hobgoblin
J - 19. JEALOUS		S. Of dubious origins
Y - 20. PECULIAR		T. Sliding feet along the floor
W - 21. VICIOUS		U. Copies
E - 22. TRIGGERS		V. Shakes or trembles
F - 23. RADIOACTIVITY		W. Savage; evil; dangerous
B - 24. ATOM		X. Sweet
U - 25. MIMEOGRAPHED		Y. Odd

Copyrighted

Gamma Rays Vocabulary Matching 3

___ 1. NERVE   A. Brazen boldness
___ 2. BERSERK   B. Time for half of nuclei to radioactively decay
___ 3. HALFLIFE   C. One who is crazy or simple-minded
___ 4. SINISTER   D. An eccentric person
___ 5. HYSTERICAL   E. Blood clot in blood vessel or heart
___ 6. TRIGGERS   F. Intense joy or delight
___ 7. PERVADES   G. Shake violently
___ 8. LOON   H. Like a machine
___ 9. SUFFOCATE   I. Soft fluttering or crackling sounds
___ 10. RUSTLING   J. Having excessive or uncontrollable emotion
___ 11. PSORIASIS   K. A skin disease
___ 12. THROMBOSIS   L. A terrifying presence; hobgoblin
___ 13. COOT   M. A change, as in nature, form, or quality
___ 14. RUMMAGES   N. Spreads throughout
___ 15. ECSTASY   O. Structure of an organism or organ
___ 16. TREMBLE   P. Shakes or trembles
___ 17. PUNCTUATES   Q. Incapability of producing offspring
___ 18. ANATOMY   R. Precipitates; causes to happen
___ 19. MECHANICALLY   S. Having qualities usually associated with females
___ 20. BOGEYMAN   T. Makes a disorderly search of
___ 21. EFFEMINATE   U. Deranged; crazed
___ 22. STERILITY   V. Kill by preventing access to oxygen
___ 23. VIBRATES   W. Threatening evil
___ 24. HORRIFIES   X. Scares; shocks; causes horror
___ 25. MUTATION   Y. Emphasizes

Gamma Rays Vocabulary Matching 3 Answer Key

A - 1. NERVE		A. Brazen boldness
U - 2. BERSERK		B. Time for half of nuclei to radioactively decay
B - 3. HALFLIFE		C. One who is crazy or simple-minded
W - 4. SINISTER		D. An eccentric person
J - 5. HYSTERICAL		E. Blood clot in blood vessel or heart
R - 6. TRIGGERS		F. Intense joy or delight
N - 7. PERVADES		G. Shake violently
C - 8. LOON		H. Like a machine
V - 9. SUFFOCATE		I. Soft fluttering or crackling sounds
I - 10. RUSTLING		J. Having excessive or uncontrollable emotion
K - 11. PSORIASIS		K. A skin disease
E - 12. THROMBOSIS		L. A terrifying presence; hobgoblin
D - 13. COOT		M. A change, as in nature, form, or quality
T - 14. RUMMAGES		N. Spreads throughout
F - 15. ECSTASY		O. Structure of an organism or organ
G - 16. TREMBLE		P. Shakes or trembles
Y - 17. PUNCTUATES		Q. Incapability of producing offspring
O - 18. ANATOMY		R. Precipitates; causes to happen
H - 19. MECHANICALLY		S. Having qualities usually associated with females
L - 20. BOGEYMAN		T. Makes a disorderly search of
S - 21. EFFEMINATE		U. Deranged; crazed
Q - 22. STERILITY		V. Kill by preventing access to oxygen
P - 23. VIBRATES		W. Threatening evil
X - 24. HORRIFIES		X. Scares; shocks; causes horror
M - 25. MUTATION		Y. Emphasizes

Gamma Rays Vocabulary Matching 4 Answer Key

1. MIMEOGRAPHED
2. CATARACTS
3. TREMBLE
4. PRIMEVAL
5. BERSERK
6. PECULIAR
7. EAVESDROPPING
8. HORRIFIES
9. MISBEGOTTEN
10. CONVULSIONS
11. TRIGGERS
12. RUMMAGES
13. ECSTASY
14. HALFLIFE
15. NERVE
16. EXAGGERATING
17. OBLIVIOUS
18. PUNCTUATES
19. BOGEYMAN
20. MUTATION
21. SUFFOCATE
22. PERVADES
23. VICIOUS
24. SACCHARINE
25. ATOM

A. Intense joy or delight
B. Sweet
C. Smallest unit of an element
D. Savage; evil; dangerous
E. Intense involuntary muscular contractions
F. A terrifying presence; hobgoblin
G. Scares; shocks; causes horror
H. Time for half of nuclei to radioactively decay
I. Spreads throughout
J. Unaware of
K. Copies
L. Emphasizes
M. Belonging to the first or earliest age or ages
N. A change, as in nature, form, or quality
O. Kill by preventing access to oxygen
P. Precipitates; causes to happen
Q. Makes a disorderly search of
R. Of dubious origins
S. Odd
T. Shake violently
U. Opacities of the eye lens or capsule
V. Enlarging, increasing beyond normal bounds
W. Listening secretly
X. Brazen boldness
Y. Deranged; crazed

Gamma Rays Vocabulary Matching 4 Answer Key

K - 1.	MIMEOGRAPHED	A. Intense joy or delight
U - 2.	CATARACTS	B. Sweet
T - 3.	TREMBLE	C. Smallest unit of an element
M - 4.	PRIMEVAL	D. Savage; evil; dangerous
Y - 5.	BERSERK	E. Intense involuntary muscular contractions
S - 6.	PECULIAR	F. A terrifying presence; hobgoblin
W - 7.	EAVESDROPPING	G. Scares; shocks; causes horror
G - 8.	HORRIFIES	H. Time for half of nuclei to radioactively decay
R - 9.	MISBEGOTTEN	I. Spreads throughout
E - 10.	CONVULSIONS	J. Unaware of
P - 11.	TRIGGERS	K. Copies
Q - 12.	RUMMAGES	L. Emphasizes
A - 13.	ECSTASY	M. Belonging to the first or earliest age or ages
H - 14.	HALFLIFE	N. A change, as in nature, form, or quality
X - 15.	NERVE	O. Kill by preventing access to oxygen
V - 16.	EXAGGERATING	P. Precipitates; causes to happen
J - 17.	OBLIVIOUS	Q. Makes a disorderly search of
L - 18.	PUNCTUATES	R. Of dubious origins
F - 19.	BOGEYMAN	S. Odd
N - 20.	MUTATION	T. Shake violently
O - 21.	SUFFOCATE	U. Opacities of the eye lens or capsule
I - 22.	PERVADES	V. Enlarging, increasing beyond normal bounds
D - 23.	VICIOUS	W. Listening secretly
B - 24.	SACCHARINE	X. Brazen boldness
C - 25.	ATOM	Y. Deranged; crazed

Gamma Rays Vocabulary Magic Squares 1

Match the definition with the vocabulary word. Put your answers in the magic squares below. When your answers are correct, all columns and rows will add to the same number.

A. COMMENCES
B. EFFEMINATE
C. FERMENT
D. EXAGGERATING
E. PSORIASIS
F. SUFFOCATE
G. CALCULATES
H. PERVADES
I. TRIGGERS
J. CHLOROFORM
K. INCONSPICUOUS
L. GASPS
M. ECSTASY
N. HYSTERICAL
O. VICIOUS
P. FLINGING

1. Kill by preventing access to oxygen
2. Precipitates; causes to happen
3. Savage; evil; dangerous
4. Enlarging, increasing beyond normal bounds
5. Intense joy or delight
6. Having qualities usually associated with females
7. Spreads throughout
8. Not readily noticeable
9. To seethe; to be agitated
10. Casting aside; discarding
11. Chemical to anesthetize or kill
12. A skin disease
13. Sharp breaths
14. Computes mathematically
15. Starts
16. Having excessive or uncontrollable emotion

A=	B=	C=	D=
E=	F=	G=	H=
I=	J=	K=	L=
M=	N=	O=	P=

Gamma Rays Vocabulary Magic Squares 1 Answer Key

Match the definition with the vocabulary word. Put your answers in the magic squares below. When your answers are correct, all columns and rows will add to the same number.

A. COMMENCES
B. EFFEMINATE
C. FERMENT
D. EXAGGERATING
E. PSORIASIS
F. SUFFOCATE
G. CALCULATES
H. PERVADES
I. TRIGGERS
J. CHLOROFORM
K. INCONSPICUOUS
L. GASPS
M. ECSTASY
N. HYSTERICAL
O. VICIOUS
P. FLINGING

1. Kill by preventing access to oxygen
2. Precipitates; causes to happen
3. Savage; evil; dangerous
4. Enlarging, increasing beyond normal bounds
5. Intense joy or delight
6. Having qualities usually associated with females
7. Spreads throughout
8. Not readily noticeable
9. To seethe; to be agitated
10. Casting aside; discarding
11. Chemical to anesthetize or kill
12. A skin disease
13. Sharp breaths
14. Computes mathematically
15. Starts
16. Having excessive or uncontrollable emotion

A=15	B=6	C=9	D=4
E=12	F=1	G=14	H=7
I=2	J=11	K=8	L=13
M=5	N=16	O=3	P=10

Gamma Rays Vocabulary Magic Squares 2

Match the definition with the vocabulary word. Put your answers in the magic squares below. When your answers are correct, all columns and rows will add to the same number.

A. SANATORIUM
B. SHUFFLING
C. FERMENT
D. SACCHARINE
E. ATOM
F. EFFEMINATE
G. PECULIAR
H. COMPETITION
I. CONVULSIONS
J. SNOOP
K. SMUG
L. SUFFOCATE
M. BERSERK
N. MISBEGOTTEN
O. BOGEYMAN
P. PERVADES

1. Of dubious origins
2. Odd
3. Kill by preventing access to oxygen
4. A place of convalescence from illness
5. Self-satisfied; complacent
6. Sliding feet along the floor
7. Deranged; crazed
8. Others capable of winning
9. Smallest unit of an element
10. Spreads throughout
11. To seethe; to be agitated
12. One who pries secretly
13. Sweet
14. Intense involuntary muscular contractions
15. Having qualities usually associated with females
16. A terrifying presence; hobgoblin

A=	B=	C=	D=
E=	F=	G=	H=
I=	J=	K=	L=
M=	N=	O=	P=

Gamma Rays Vocabulary Magic Squares 2 Answer Key

Match the definition with the vocabulary word. Put your answers in the magic squares below. When your answers are correct, all columns and rows will add to the same number.

A. SANATORIUM
B. SHUFFLING
C. FERMENT
D. SACCHARINE
E. ATOM
F. EFFEMINATE
G. PECULIAR
H. COMPETITION
I. CONVULSIONS
J. SNOOP
K. SMUG
L. SUFFOCATE
M. BERSERK
N. MISBEGOTTEN
O. BOGEYMAN
P. PERVADES

1. Of dubious origins
2. Odd
3. Kill by preventing access to oxygen
4. A place of convalescence from illness
5. Self-satisfied; complacent
6. Sliding feet along the floor
7. Deranged; crazed
8. Others capable of winning
9. Smallest unit of an element
10. Spreads throughout
11. To seethe; to be agitated
12. One who pries secretly
13. Sweet
14. Intense involuntary muscular contractions
15. Having qualities usually associated with females
16. A terrifying presence; hobgoblin

A=4	B=6	C=11	D=13
E=9	F=15	G=2	H=8
I=14	J=12	K=5	L=3
M=7	N=1	O=16	P=10

Gamma Rays Vocabulary Magic Squares 3

Match the definition with the vocabulary word. Put your answers in the magic squares below. When your answers are correct, all columns and rows will add to the same number.

A. LOON
B. ACCENTUATED
C. TREMBLE
D. PATHETIC
E. CALCULATES
F. FLINGING
G. SUFFOCATE
H. JEALOUS
I. MUTATION
J. STAGGERING
K. HALFLIFE
L. FERMENT
M. TRANSPLANT
N. MIMEOGRAPHED
O. ATOM
P. BERSERK

1. Uproot and replant
2. Casting aside; discarding
3. Envious
4. Smallest unit of an element
5. To seethe; to be agitated
6. Shake violently
7. One who is crazy or simple-minded
8. Overwhelming
9. Time for half of nuclei to radioactively decay
10. Arousing sympathy and compassion
11. Stressed; accented
12. A change, as in nature, form, or quality
13. Copies
14. Computes mathematically
15. Kill by preventing access to oxygen
16. Deranged; crazed

A=	B=	C=	D=
E=	F=	G=	H=
I=	J=	K=	L=
M=	N=	O=	P=

Gamma Rays Vocabulary magic Squares 3 Answer Key

Match the definition with the vocabulary word. Put your answers in the magic squares below. When your answers are correct, all columns and rows will add to the same number.

A. LOON
B. ACCENTUATED
C. TREMBLE
D. PATHETIC
E. CALCULATES
F. FLINGING
G. SUFFOCATE
H. JEALOUS
I. MUTATION
J. STAGGERING
K. HALFLIFE
L. FERMENT
M. TRANSPLANT
N. MIMEOGRAPHED
O. ATOM
P. BERSERK

1. Uproot and replant
2. Casting aside; discarding
3. Envious
4. Smallest unit of an element
5. To seethe; to be agitated
6. Shake violently
7. One who is crazy or simple-minded
8. Overwhelming
9. Time for half of nuclei to radioactively decay
10. Arousing sympathy and compassion
11. Stressed; accented
12. A change, as in nature, form, or quality
13. Copies
14. Computes mathematically
15. Kill by preventing access to oxygen
16. Deranged; crazed

A=7	B=11	C=6	D=10
E=14	F=2	G=15	H=3
I=12	J=8	K=9	L=5
M=1	N=13	O=4	P=16

Gamma Rays Vocabulary Magic Squares 4

Match the definition with the vocabulary word. Put your answers in the magic squares below. When your answers are correct, all columns and rows will add to the same number.

A. SILHOUETTE
B. SMUG
C. TRANSPLANT
D. CONVULSIONS
E. PRIMEVAL
F. SNOOP
G. BOGEYMAN
H. PERVADES
I. GASPS
J. ANCIENT
K. THROMBOSIS
L. MUTATION
M. TRIGGERS
N. RADIOACTIVITY
O. EFFEMINATE
P. PECULIAR

1. Outline or profile
2. Spontaneous emission of radiation
3. Very old
4. Belonging to the first or earliest age or ages
5. A terrifying presence; hobgoblin
6. A change, as in nature, form, or quality
7. Odd
8. Uproot and replant
9. Having qualities usually associated with females
10. Intense involuntary muscular contractions
11. Spreads throughout
12. Blood clot in blood vessel or heart
13. Sharp breaths
14. One who pries secretly
15. Self-satisfied; complacent
16. Precipitates; causes to happen

A=	B=	C=	D=
E=	F=	G=	H=
I=	J=	K=	L=
M=	N=	O=	P=

Gamma Rays Vocabulary Magic Squares 4 Answer Key

Match the definition with the vocabulary word. Put your answers in the magic squares below. When your answers are correct, all columns and rows will add to the same number.

A. SILHOUETTE
B. SMUG
C. TRANSPLANT
D. CONVULSIONS
E. PRIMEVAL
F. SNOOP

G. BOGEYMAN
H. PERVADES
I. GASPS
J. ANCIENT
K. THROMBOSIS
L. MUTATION

M. TRIGGERS
N. RADIOACTIVITY
O. EFFEMINATE
P. PECULIAR

1. Outline or profile
2. Spontaneous emission of radiation
3. Very old
4. Belonging to the first or earliest age or ages
5. A terrifying presence; hobgoblin
6. A change, as in nature, form, or quality
7. Odd
8. Uproot and replant
9. Having qualities usually associated with females
10. Intense involuntary muscular contractions
11. Spreads throughout
12. Blood clot in blood vessel or heart
13. Sharp breaths
14. One who pries secretly
15. Self-satisfied; complacent
16. Precipitates; causes to happen

A=1	B=15	C=8	D=10
E=4	F=14	G=5	H=11
I=13	J=3	K=12	L=6
M=16	N=2	O=9	P=7

Gamma Rays Vocabulary Word Search 1

```
T P C A L C U L A T E S M W T K S N R J
H R H B R U M M A G E S T G R Q N S U J
R I J C V I C I O U S Y B Q I F O M S S
O M Z E O F E R M E N T M O G C O U T D
M E C H A N I C A L L Y Z Z G X P G L W
B V A G C L V N S T J V P N E E D Y I K
O A X V C S O U C T W Y I R R G Y J N F
S L G A E B U U L L A L F R S N K M G G
I H B N N S Z F S S F S L G U I E T A H
S C W A T L D K F F I A Y K O R T R B N
K A O T U R J R U O C O X B I E E A V Y
P T M O A G E H O I C S N K V G R N P E
T A U M T A S M R P E A R S I G N S E V
W R T Y E S W E B D P E T X L A I P C P
Z A A H D P T K A L S I V E B T T L U F
F C T Q E S L V X R E D N L O S Y A L J
J T I F Y T R S E K N Z C G Z P M N I V
T S O H N E I B C O M M E N C E S T A V
M N N R P G N C O L C H L O R O F O R M
A N C I E N T L F L I N G I N G K J D T
```

A change, as in nature, form, or quality (8)
A terrifying presence; hobgoblin (8)
An eccentric person (4)
Arousing sympathy and compassion (8)
Belonging to the first or earliest age or ages (8)
Blood clot in blood vessel or heart (10)
Brazen boldness (5)
Casting aside; discarding (8)
Chemical to anesthetize or kill (10)
Continuance without beginning or end (8)
Deranged; crazed (7)
Envious (7)
Having excessive or uncontrollable emotion (10)
Intense involuntary muscular contractions (11)
Intense joy or delight (7)
Kill by preventing access to oxygen (9)
Like a machine (12)
Listening secretly (13)
Makes a disorderly search of (8)
Odd (8)
One who is crazy or simple-minded (4)

One who pries secretly (5)
Opacities of the eye lens or capsule (9)
Overwhelming (10)
Precipitates; causes to happen (8)
Savage; evil; dangerous (7)
Self-satisfied; complacent (4)
Shake violently (7)
Sharp breaths (5)
Sliding feet along the floor (9)
Smallest unit of an element (4)
Soft fluttering or crackling sounds (8)
Spreads throughout (8)
Starts (9)
Stressed; accented (11)
Structure of an organism or organ (7)
To seethe; to be agitated (7)
Unaware of (9)
Uproot and replant (10)
Very old (7)
Computes mathematically (10)

Gamma Rays Vocabulary Word Search 1 Answer Key

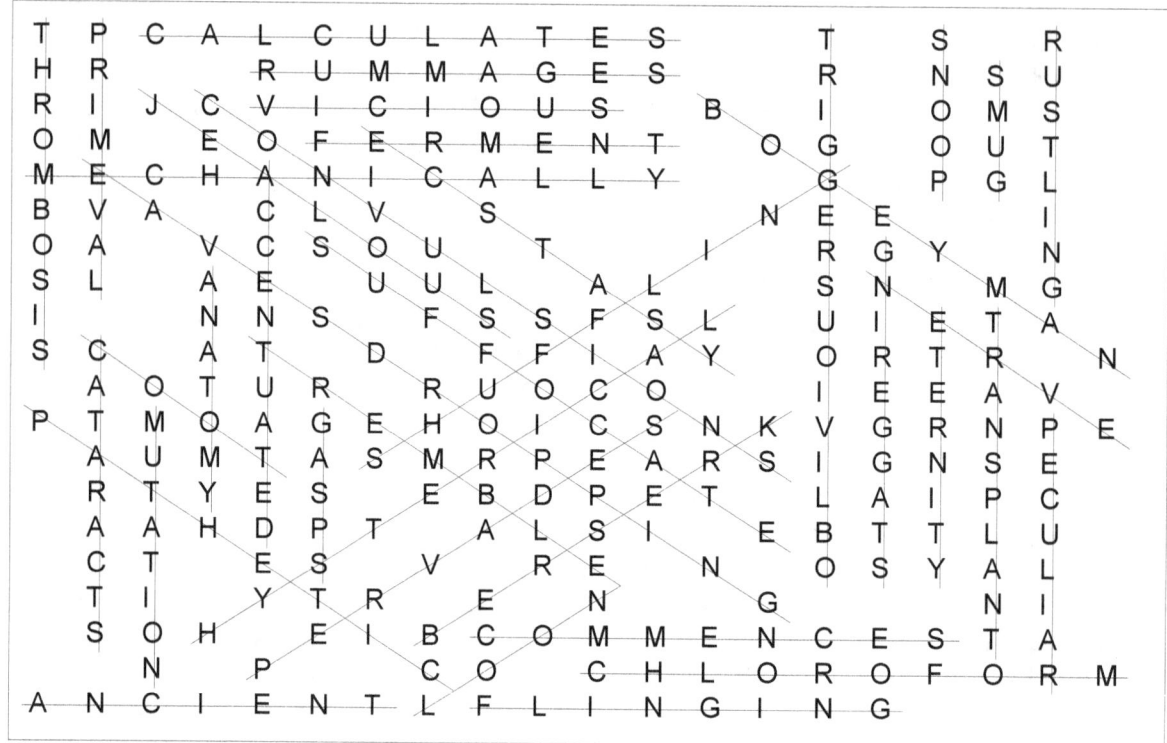

A change, as in nature, form, or quality (8)
A terrifying presence; hobgoblin (8)
An eccentric person (4)
Arousing sympathy and compassion (8)
Belonging to the first or earliest age or ages (8)
Blood clot in blood vessel or heart (10)
Brazen boldness (5)
Casting aside; discarding (8)
Chemical to anesthetize or kill (10)
Continuance without beginning or end (8)
Deranged; crazed (7)
Envious (7)
Having excessive or uncontrollable emotion (10)
Intense involuntary muscular contractions (11)
Intense joy or delight (7)
Kill by preventing access to oxygen (9)
Like a machine (12)
Listening secretly (13)
Makes a disorderly search of (8)
Odd (8)
One who is crazy or simple-minded (4)

One who pries secretly (5)
Opacities of the eye lens or capsule (9)
Overwhelming (10)
Precipitates; causes to happen (8)
Savage; evil; dangerous (7)
Self-satisfied; complacent (4)
Shake violently (7)
Sharp breaths (5)
Sliding feet along the floor (9)
Smallest unit of an element (4)
Soft fluttering or crackling sounds (8)
Spreads throughout (8)
Starts (9)
Stressed; accented (11)
Structure of an organism or organ (7)
To seethe; to be agitated (7)
Unaware of (9)
Uproot and replant (10)
Very old (7)
Computes mathematically (10)

Gamma Rays Vocabulary Word Search 2

```
S W L W P Q E C S T A S Y S W V J P R K
T H N O S V I C I O U S U E V Y S U U N
C N N Z O W C H L O R O F O R M I N S N
A O T M R N D Z L W U I F A U O N C T L
R T O O I W C A P C L Y I G M T I L T
A R Y T A P E A I F D L S A M A S U I H
T E F A S J Z P L S U S N N A N T A N M
A M E Z I J S A U C E J O C G A E T G F
C B R D S N H O E C U I O I E C R E P D
V L M X O H I P N T T L P E S Y S S E X
I E E C Z V O E H I R L A N Z Y Y H R N
B L N V I M M R T P A I H T E Q P B V M
R I T L Q M O E R C A G G V E A K E A S
A R B D O M P V I I N T R G R S M R D K
T O X C B M M R G I F U H G E Z H S E L
E P B O O V E E G C S I O E T R W E S X
S K S C Y T I N R E T E E F T X S R X T
J I X Z S S I D D S M F H S J I M K T X
S T Q Y Y L L A C I N A H C E M C Z X F
J Y H T F C N A M Y E G O B G A S P S L
```

A skin disease (9)
A terrifying presence; hobgoblin (8)
An eccentric person (4)
Arousing sympathy and compassion (8)
Blood clot in blood vessel or heart (10)
Brazen boldness (5)
Casting aside; discarding (8)
Chemical to anesthetize or kill (10)
Continuance without beginning or end (8)
Copies (12)
Deranged; crazed (7)
Emphasizes (10)
Envious (7)
Examines; looks at comprehensively (7)
Having excessive or uncontrollable emotion (10)
Intense joy or delight (7)
Like a machine (12)
Makes a disorderly search of (8)
Not readily noticeable (13)
Odd (8)
One who is crazy or simple-minded (4)
One who pries secretly (5)
Opacities of the eye lens or capsule (9)

Others capable of winning (11)
Precipitates; causes to happen (8)
Savage; evil; dangerous (7)
Scares; shocks; causes horror (9)
Self-satisfied; complacent (4)
Shake violently (7)
Shakes or trembles (8)
Sharp breaths (5)
Smallest unit of an element (4)
Soft fluttering or crackling sounds (8)
Spreads throughout (8)
Starts (9)
Structure of an organism or organ (7)
Threatening evil (8)
Time for half of nuclei to radioactively decay (8)
To seethe; to be agitated (7)
Unaware of (9)
Very old (7)
Computes mathematically (10)

Gamma Rays Vocabulary Word Search 2 Answer Key

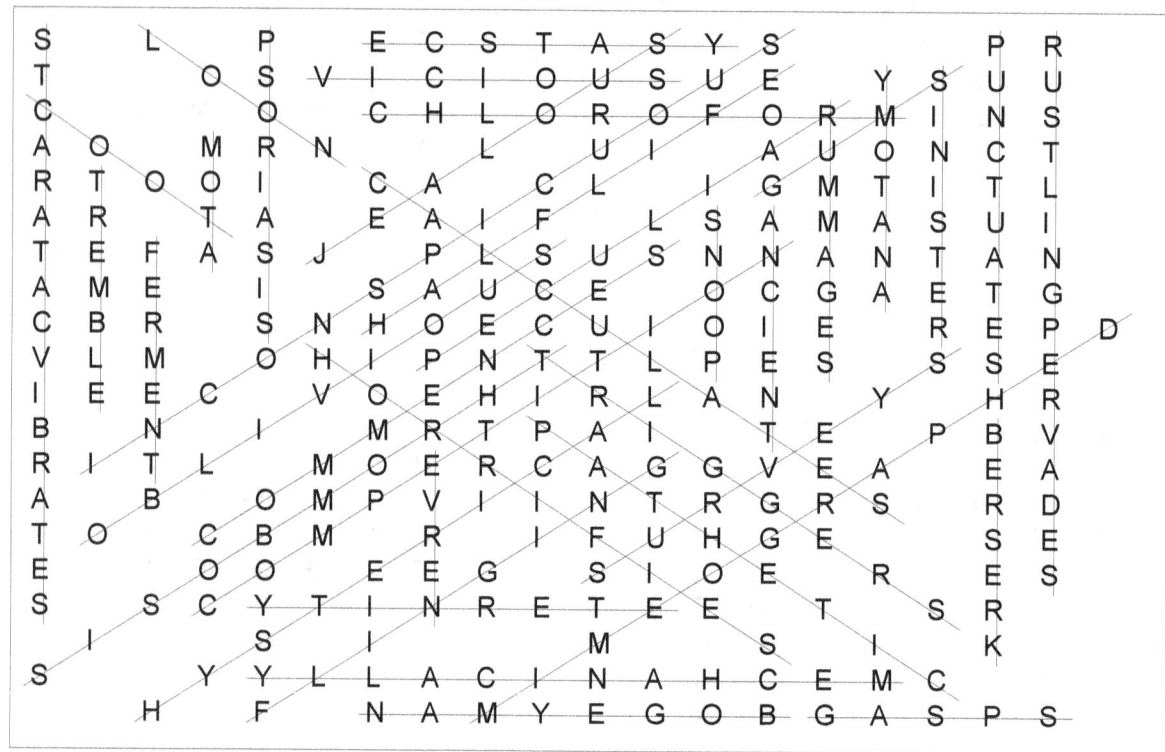

A skin disease (9)
A terrifying presence; hobgoblin (8)
An eccentric person (4)
Arousing sympathy and compassion (8)
Blood clot in blood vessel or heart (10)
Brazen boldness (5)
Casting aside; discarding (8)
Chemical to anesthetize or kill (10)
Continuance without beginning or end (8)
Copies (12)
Deranged; crazed (7)
Emphasizes (10)
Envious (7)
Examines; looks at comprehensively (7)
Having excessive or uncontrollable emotion (10)
Intense joy or delight (7)
Like a machine (12)
Makes a disorderly search of (8)
Not readily noticeable (13)
Odd (8)
One who is crazy or simple-minded (4)
One who pries secretly (5)
Opacities of the eye lens or capsule (9)

Others capable of winning (11)
Precipitates; causes to happen (8)
Savage; evil; dangerous (7)
Scares; shocks; causes horror (9)
Self-satisfied; complacent (4)
Shake violently (7)
Shakes or trembles (8)
Sharp breaths (5)
Smallest unit of an element (4)
Soft fluttering or crackling sounds (8)
Spreads throughout (8)
Starts (9)
Structure of an organism or organ (7)
Threatening evil (8)
Time for half of nuclei to radioactively decay (8)
To seethe; to be agitated (7)
Unaware of (9)
Very old (7)
Computes mathematically (10)

Gamma Rays Vocabulary Word Search 3

```
I N C O N S P I C U O U S E C S T A S Y N H O E M
P H J R C L G I E B R V H R M X B C B A E Y B X I
H R L E S O T G D A W T L K O Q B K O N R S L A S
O S I Y A E M R X J V R U S T L I N G A V T I S B
R C V M H L E M S Z Q E A S A N D X E T E E V P E
R Z T T E T O T E C B M S N U D V Y Y O V R I E G
I X A A S V C U A N S B B D C R T C M M I I O R O
F P S I C A A L S I C L E E R I V Z A Y C C U A T
I P N V R C C L S E N E N R V O E E N G I A S T T
E I U A I U E A D T F I S I S V P N Y W O L I E E
S T T N L B I N N D R F T T F E K P T S U R S P N
B A E A C R R A T A M C E R G K R G I N S V O Q R
C S T R O T L A H U A V E M Z T N K W N R Q B U Q
X E V S N P U C T O A F B Y I I R V T A G R M Y F
S D P C S I C A I E I T R C L N F I I N W M O E Q
R A W N V A T D T L S S E F X V A L G F A Z R L V
D V A F S I A Y F E N M F D H S U T C G B M H O T
M R O F O R O L H C S U F F O C A T E N E V T O L
T E P N T C A B B K H G H W E P H S J N T R O N G
Z P P T B H H G A S P S Q P O O N S T L W C S Y D
```

ACCENTUATED	GASPS	RADIOACTIVITY
ANATOMY	HALFLIFE	RUMMAGES
ANCIENT	HORRIFIES	RUSTLING
ATOM	HYSTERICAL	SACCHARINE
BERSERK	INCONSPICUOUS	SHUFFLING
BOGEYMAN	JEALOUS	SINISTER
CALCULATES	LOON	SMUG
CATARACTS	MISBEGOTTEN	SNOOP
CHLOROFORM	MUTATION	SUFFOCATE
COMMENCES	NERVE	SURVEYS
COOT	OBLIVIOUS	THROMBOSIS
EAVESDROPPING	PATHETIC	TRANSPLANT
ECSTASY	PECULIAR	TREMBLE
EFFEMINATE	PERVADES	TRIGGERS
ETERNITY	PRIMEVAL	VIBRATES
EXASPERATE	PSORIASIS	VICIOUS
FERMENT	PUNCTUATES	

Gamma Rays Vocabulary Word Search 3 Answer Key

ACCENTUATED	GASPS	RADIOACTIVITY
ANATOMY	HALFLIFE	RUMMAGES
ANCIENT	HORRIFIES	RUSTLING
ATOM	HYSTERICAL	SACCHARINE
BERSERK	INCONSPICUOUS	SHUFFLING
BOGEYMAN	JEALOUS	SINISTER
CALCULATES	LOON	SMUG
CATARACTS	MISBEGOTTEN	SNOOP
CHLOROFORM	MUTATION	SUFFOCATE
COMMENCES	NERVE	SURVEYS
COOT	OBLIVIOUS	THROMBOSIS
EAVESDROPPING	PATHETIC	TRANSPLANT
ECSTASY	PECULIAR	TREMBLE
EFFEMINATE	PERVADES	TRIGGERS
ETERNITY	PRIMEVAL	VIBRATES
EXASPERATE	PSORIASIS	VICIOUS
FERMENT	PUNCTUATES	

Gamma Rays Vocabulary Word Search 4

```
F V I B R A T E S F S U F F O C A T E X S C L Z Y
L L B S E Z G P W M U N T S D K R N W K U O O X J
S G I P H R L K D S O D O N T E P E W M O O O D L
A A M N X U S F Y E I P H O M T A I X H L T N G B
C S S T G X F E B P C T M B P S T C A R A T A C T
C P F R J I V F R S I S L Z E F H N X G E Y D Y G
H S K A X R N R L K V E T C R L E A X L J E D N J
A V S N U R X G B I Y P N A Q Y T P P L H Q I N W
R E T S I N I S P M N E E X S P I D D P Z T P A D
I R T P Q B C Y O E M G M C H Y C G A J A B U M C
N U R L S Y P T R M K M R B U N N R E R F J N Y S
E S I A E G A V O V L B E V O L G F E P H D C E A
W T G N G N E C K S V K F I J O I G B O C W T G N
F L G T A P Q Y E L Y F T M E L G A R F F A U O A
W I E Y M K C D A K D A W M F A Z R R Q L Z A B T
J N R L M K A K T S T W I L X W I S M U T F T B O
V G S S U V L S O U N M A E D F F V C D S D E S R
Y T I N R E T E M E C H A N I C A L L Y B M S W I
L A V E M I R P H G N I R E G G A T S D T T U M U
T L P T H R O M B O S I S L A C I R E T S Y H G M
```

ANATOMY
ANCIENT
ATOM
BERSERK
BOGEYMAN
CALCULATES
CATARACTS
COMMENCES
COOT
ECSTASY
ETERNITY
EXAGGERATING
FERMENT
FLINGING
GASPS
HALFLIFE

HORRIFIES
HYSTERICAL
JEALOUS
LOON
MECHANICALLY
MIMEOGRAPHED
MUTATION
NERVE
PATHETIC
PECULIAR
PERVADES
PRIMEVAL
PUNCTUATES
RUMMAGES
RUSTLING
SACCHARINE

SANATORIUM
SHUFFLING
SINISTER
SMUG
SNOOP
STAGGERING
SUFFOCATE
SURVEYS
THROMBOSIS
TRANSPLANT
TREMBLE
TRIGGERS
VIBRATES
VICIOUS

Gamma Rays Vocabulary Word Search 4 Answer Key

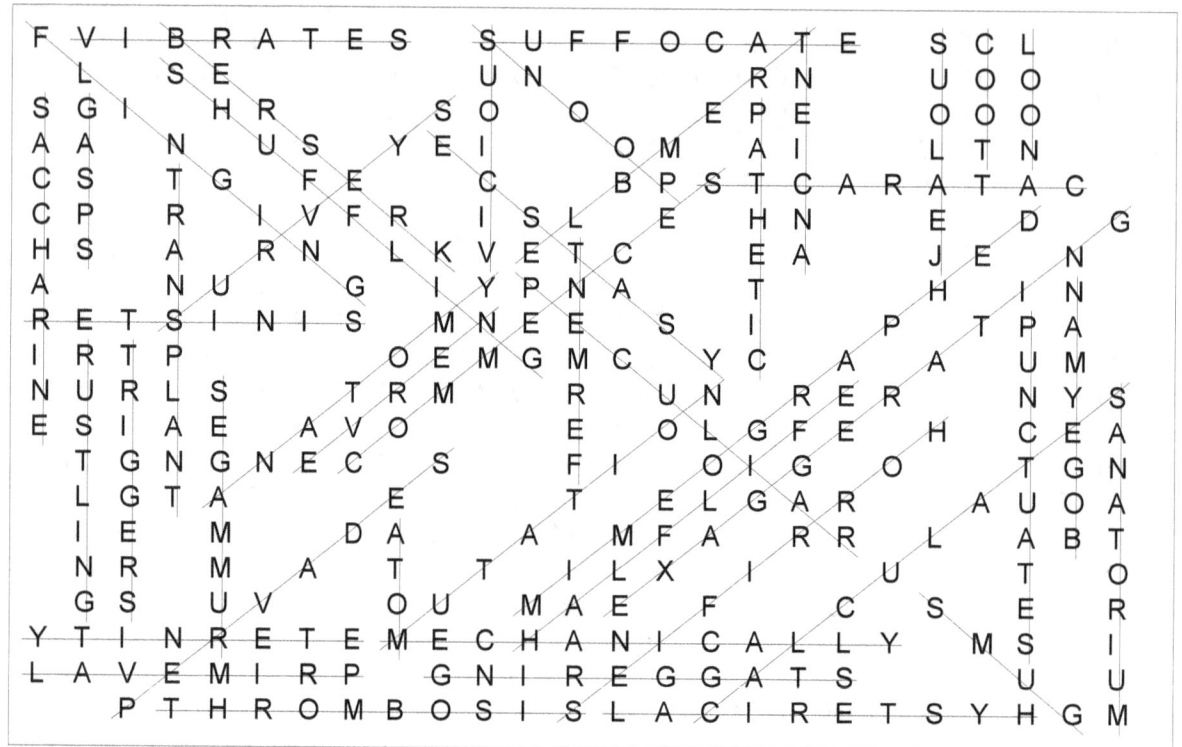

ANATOMY	HORRIFIES	SANATORIUM
ANCIENT	HYSTERICAL	SHUFFLING
ATOM	JEALOUS	SINISTER
BERSERK	LOON	SMUG
BOGEYMAN	MECHANICALLY	SNOOP
CALCULATES	MIMEOGRAPHED	STAGGERING
CATARACTS	MUTATION	SUFFOCATE
COMMENCES	NERVE	SURVEYS
COOT	PATHETIC	THROMBOSIS
ECSTASY	PECULIAR	TRANSPLANT
ETERNITY	PERVADES	TREMBLE
EXAGGERATING	PRIMEVAL	TRIGGERS
FERMENT	PUNCTUATES	VIBRATES
FLINGING	RUMMAGES	VICIOUS
GASPS	RUSTLING	
HALFLIFE	SACCHARINE	

Gamma Rays Vocabulary Crossword 1

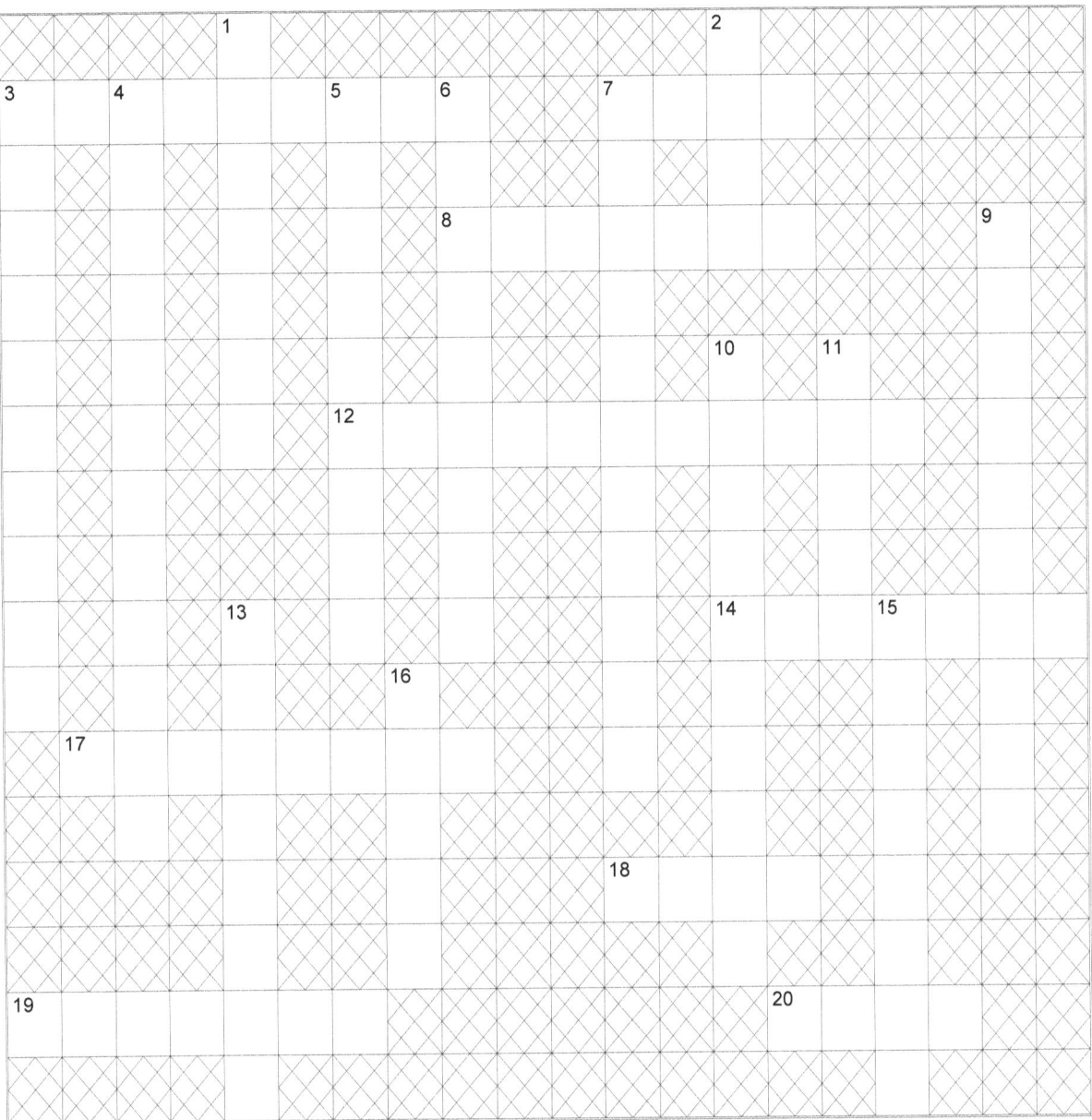

Across
3. Starts
7. An eccentric person
8. To seethe; to be agitated
12. Stressed; accented
14. Shake violently
17. Casting aside; discarding
18. Self-satisfied; complacent
19. Examines; looks at comprehensively
20. Smallest unit of an element

Down
1. Deranged; crazed
2. One who is crazy or simple-minded
3. Chemical to anesthetize or kill
4. Like a machine
5. Opacities of the eye lens or capsule
6. Kill by preventing access to oxygen
7. Others capable of winning
9. Uproot and replant
10. A place of convalescence from illness
11. Brazen boldness
13. Threatening evil
15. A change, as in nature, form, or quality
16. One who pries secretly

Gamma Rays Vocabulary Crossword 1 Answer Key

Across
- 3. Starts
- 7. An eccentric person
- 8. To seethe; to be agitated
- 12. Stressed; accented
- 14. Shake violently
- 17. Casting aside; discarding
- 18. Self-satisfied; complacent
- 19. Examines; looks at comprehensively
- 20. Smallest unit of an element

Down
- 1. Deranged; crazed
- 2. One who is crazy or simple-minded
- 3. Chemical to anesthetize or kill
- 4. Like a machine
- 5. Opacities of the eye lens or capsule
- 6. Kill by preventing access to oxygen
- 7. Others capable of winning
- 9. Uproot and replant
- 10. A place of convalescence from illness
- 11. Brazen boldness
- 13. Threatening evil
- 15. A change, as in nature, form, or quality
- 16. One who pries secretly

Across answers: 3. COMMENCES, 7. COOT, 8. FERMENT, 12. ACCENTUATED, 14. TREMBLE, 17. FLINGING, 18. SMUG, 19. SURVEYS, 20. ATOM

Down answers: 1. BEASTARFOOPM (B...), 2. LOON, 3. CHLOROFORM, 4. MECHANICAL, 5. CATARACTS, 6. SUFFOCATE, 7. CONTENTIONS, 9. TRANSPLANT, 10. SANATORIUM, 11. INVERT, 13. SINISTER, 15. MUTATION, 16. SNOOP

Gamma Rays Vocabulary Crossword 2

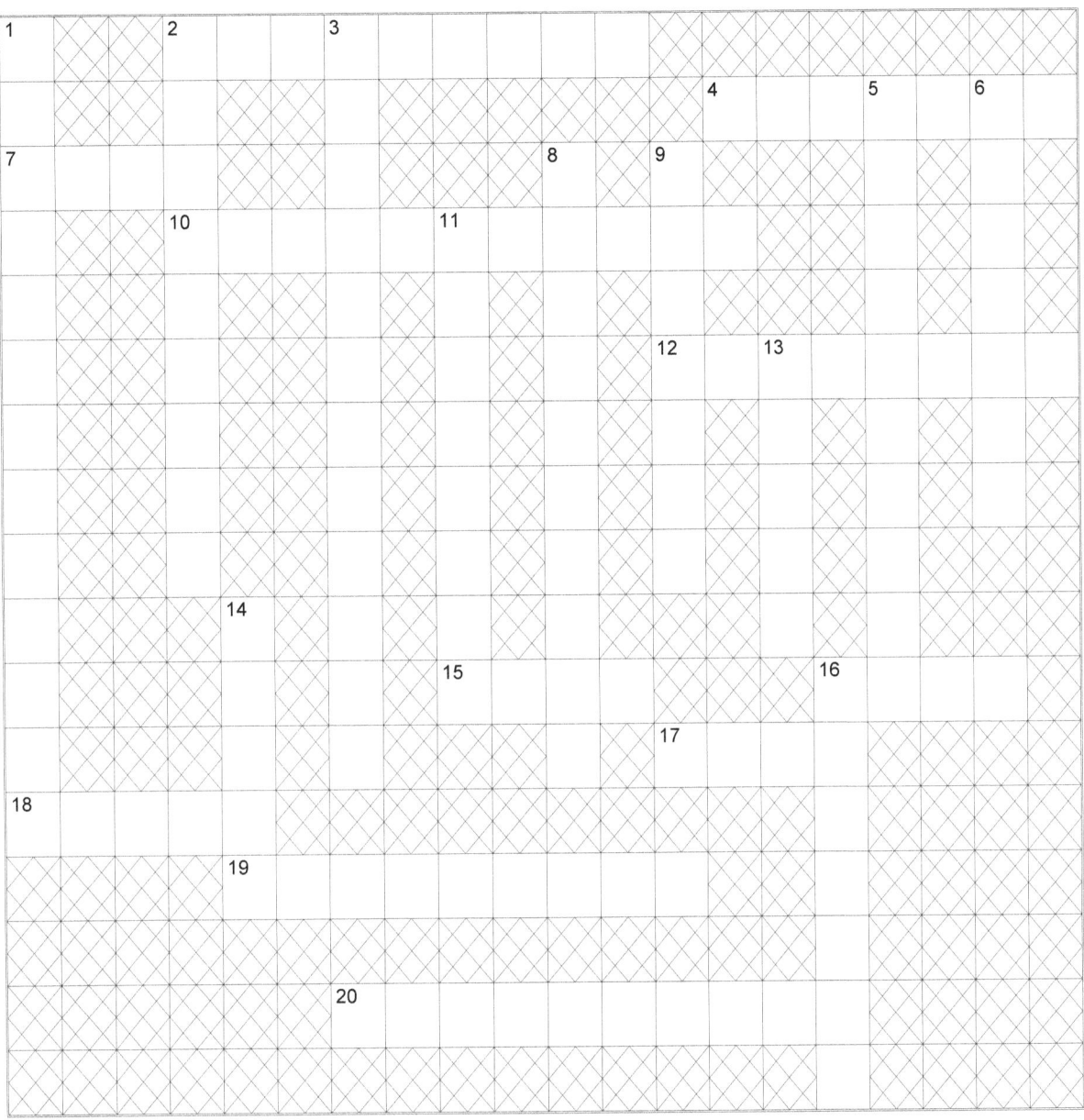

Across
2. Starts
4. Intense joy or delight
7. An eccentric person
10. Stressed; accented
12. Threatening evil
15. Self-satisfied; complacent
16. Smallest unit of an element
17. One who is crazy or simple-minded
18. One who pries secretly
19. Kill by preventing access to oxygen
20. Chemical to anesthetize or kill

Down
1. Not readily noticeable
2. Opacities of the eye lens or capsule
3. Copies
5. Uproot and replant
6. Examines; looks at comprehensively
8. A place of convalescence from illness
9. Deranged; crazed
11. Precipitates; causes to happen
13. Brazen boldness
14. Sharp breaths
16. Structure of an organism or organ

Gamma Rays Vocabulary Crossword 2 Answer Key

	1		2		3								
	I		C	O	M	M	E	N	C	E	S		
	N		A		I					4		5	6
	N		A		I					E	C S	T	A S Y
7							8	9					
C	O	O	T		M		S	B				R	U
	O		10			11						A	R
			A	C	C	E	N	T	U	A T E	D	A	R
	N		R		O		R	N		R		N	V
	S		A		G		I	A		12	13		
	S		A		G		I	A		S I N	I	S T	E R
	P		C		R		G	T		E		N	P	Y
	I		T		A		G	O		R		R	L	S
	C		S		P		E	R		K		V	A
			14										
	U		G		H		R	I				E	N
						15						16	
	O		A		E		S	M	U	G		A T O M
	U		S		D			M		17		
	U		S		D			M		L O O	N	
	18											
	S	N	O	O	P					A		
					19							
					S	U	F	F	O	C A T	E	
										O		
					20							
					C	H	L	O	R	O F O	R M	
											Y	

Across
- 2. Starts
- 4. Intense joy or delight
- 7. An eccentric person
- 10. Stressed; accented
- 12. Threatening evil
- 15. Self-satisfied; complacent
- 16. Smallest unit of an element
- 17. One who is crazy or simple-minded
- 18. One who pries secretly
- 19. Kill by preventing access to oxygen
- 20. Chemical to anesthetize or kill

Down
- 1. Not readily noticeable
- 2. Opacities of the eye lens or capsule
- 3. Copies
- 5. Uproot and replant
- 6. Examines; looks at comprehensively
- 8. A place of convalescence from illness
- 9. Deranged; crazed
- 11. Precipitates; causes to happen
- 13. Brazen boldness
- 14. Sharp breaths
- 16. Structure of an organism or organ

Gamma Rays Vocabulary Crossword 3

Across
2. Savage; evil; dangerous
5. Precipitates; causes to happen
6. One who is crazy or simple-minded
8. Starts
10. A change, as in nature, form, or quality
13. Stressed; accented
16. Threatening evil
17. Self-satisfied; complacent

Down
1. Deranged; crazed
2. Shakes or trembles
3. Others capable of winning
4. One who pries secretly
5. Shake violently
7. Brazen boldness
8. Opacities of the eye lens or capsule
9. Intense involuntary muscular contractions
10. Of dubious origins
11. Incapability of producing offspring
12. Time for half of nuclei to radioactively decay
14. An eccentric person
15. Odd
16. Examines; looks at comprehensively

Gamma Rays Vocabulary Crossword 3 Answer Key

Across
2. Savage; evil; dangerous
5. Precipitates; causes to happen
6. One who is crazy or simple-minded
8. Starts
10. A change, as in nature, form, or quality
13. Stressed; accented
16. Threatening evil
17. Self-satisfied; complacent

Down
1. Deranged; crazed
2. Shakes or trembles
3. Others capable of winning
4. One who pries secretly
5. Shake violently
7. Brazen boldness
8. Opacities of the eye lens or capsule
9. Intense involuntary muscular contractions
10. Of dubious origins
11. Incapability of producing offspring
12. Time for half of nuclei to radioactively decay
14. An eccentric person
15. Odd
16. Examines; looks at comprehensively

Gamma Rays Vocabulary Crossword 4

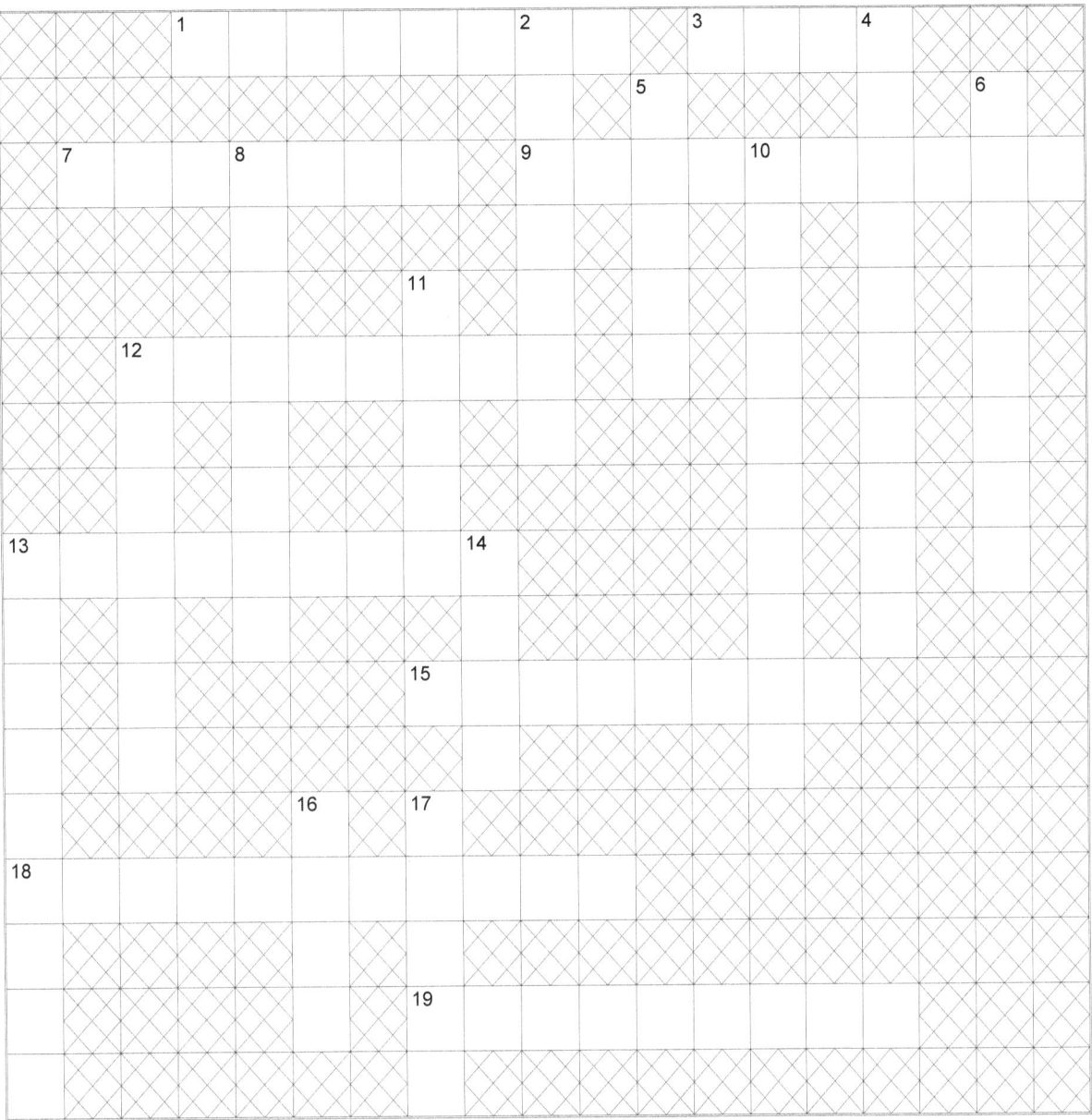

Across
1. Shakes or trembles
3. An eccentric person
7. Deranged; crazed
9. A place of convalescence from illness
12. Precipitates; causes to happen
13. Starts
15. Soft fluttering or crackling sounds
18. Stressed; accented
19. A skin disease

Down
2. Intense joy or delight
4. Blood clot in blood vessel or heart
5. One who pries secretly
6. Makes a disorderly search of
8. Threatening evil
10. Uproot and replant
11. Brazen boldness
12. Shake violently
13. Opacities of the eye lens or capsule
14. Self-satisfied; complacent
16. Smallest unit of an element
17. Sharp breaths

Gamma Rays Vocabulary Crossword 4 Answer Key

Across
1. Shakes or trembles
3. An eccentric person
7. Deranged; crazed
9. A place of convalescence from illness
12. Precipitates; causes to happen
13. Starts
15. Soft fluttering or crackling sounds
18. Stressed; accented
19. A skin disease

Down
2. Intense joy or delight
4. Blood clot in blood vessel or heart
5. One who pries secretly
6. Makes a disorderly search of
8. Threatening evil
10. Uproot and replant
11. Brazen boldness
12. Shake violently
13. Opacities of the eye lens or capsule
14. Self-satisfied; complacent
16. Smallest unit of an element
17. Sharp breaths

Answers filled in grid:
- 1A VIBRATES
- 3A COOT
- 7A BERSERK
- 9A SANATORIUM
- 12A TRIGGERS
- 13A COMMENCES
- 15A RUSTLING
- 18A ACCENTUATED
- 19A PSORIASIS
- 2D ECSTASY
- 4D THROMBOSIS
- 5D SNOOP
- 6D RUMMAGE
- 8D SINISTER
- 10D TRANSPLANT
- 11D EFFRONTERY
- 12D TREMBLES
- 13D CATARACTS
- 14D SMUG
- 16D ATOM
- 17D GASPS

Gamma Rays Vocabulary Juggle Letters 1

1. RAAASTCTC = 1. _____
Opacities of the eye lens or capsule

2. EISCRHNAAC = 2. _____
Sweet

3. TAONTIUM = 3. _____
A change, as in nature, form, or quality

4. YOAMBNGE = 4. _____
A terrifying presence; hobgoblin

5. RUSSVYE = 5. _____
Examines; looks at comprehensively

6. ISESTINR = 6. _____
Threatening evil

7. SRIHCYLETA = 7. _____
Having excessive or uncontrollable emotion

8. GAPIHRMEDOME = 8. _____
Copies

9. GFSUHLFNI = 9. _____
Sliding feet along the floor

10. IMANRUTOAS =10. _____
A place of convalescence from illness

11. GGNFIINL =11. _____
Casting aside; discarding

12. RINETYTE =12. _____
Continuance without beginning or end

13. EACETANUCTD =13. _____
Stressed; accented

14. USGM =14. _____
Self-satisfied; complacent

15. AVORITIDAIYCT =15. _____
Spontaneous emission of radiation

Gamma Rays Vocabulary Juggle Letters 1 Answer Key

1. RAAASTCTC = 1. CATARACTS
Opacities of the eye lens or capsule

2. EISCRHNAAC = 2. SACCHARINE
Sweet

3. TAONTIUM = 3. MUTATION
A change, as in nature, form, or quality

4. YOAMBNGE = 4. BOGEYMAN
A terrifying presence; hobgoblin

5. RUSSVYE = 5. SURVEYS
Examines; looks at comprehensively

6. ISESTINR = 6. SINISTER
Threatening evil

7. SRIHCYLETA = 7. HYSTERICAL
Having excessive or uncontrollable emotion

8. GAPIHRMEDOME = 8. MIMEOGRAPHED
Copies

9. GFSUHLFNI = 9. SHUFFLING
Sliding feet along the floor

10. IMANRUTOAS =10. SANATORIUM
A place of convalescence from illness

11. GGNFIINL =11. FLINGING
Casting aside; discarding

12. RINETYTE =12. ETERNITY
Continuance without beginning or end

13. EACETANUCTD =13. ACCENTUATED
Stressed; accented

14. USGM =14. SMUG
Self-satisfied; complacent

15. AVORITIDAIYCT =15. RADIOACTIVITY
Spontaneous emission of radiation

Gamma Rays Vocabulary Juggle Letters 2

1. SPGAS = 1. _____
   Sharp breaths

2. ATUCUPNETS = 2. _____
   Emphasizes

3. OILNOUCNSVS = 3. _____
   Intense involuntary muscular contractions

4. MRUSAEGM = 4. _____
   Makes a disorderly search of

5. STEEMTBINOG = 5. _____
   Of dubious origins

6. LASPNTNTRA = 6. _____
   Uproot and replant

7. GUTNRLSI = 7. _____
   Soft fluttering or crackling sounds

8. OUSVCII = 8. _____
   Savage; evil; dangerous

9. IGNFINLG = 9. _____
   Casting aside; discarding

10. NSSOIONUUPCCI =10. _____
    Not readily noticeable

11. NFFTEEEMIA =11. _____
    Having qualities usually associated with females

12. VIITTCRAIOADY =12. _____
    Spontaneous emission of radiation

13. AILUCEPR =13. _____
    Odd

14. UGMS =14. _____
    Self-satisfied; complacent

15. AEHLILFF =15. _____
    Time for half of nuclei to radioactively decay

Gamma Rays Vocabulary Juggle Letters 2 Answer Key

1. SPGAS = 1. GASPS
Sharp breaths

2. ATUCUPNETS = 2. PUNCTUATES
Emphasizes

3. OILNOUCNSVS = 3. CONVULSIONS
Intense involuntary muscular contractions

4. MRUSAEGM = 4. RUMMAGES
Makes a disorderly search of

5. STEEMTBINOG = 5. MISBEGOTTEN
Of dubious origins

6. LASPNTNTRA = 6. TRANSPLANT
Uproot and replant

7. GUTNRLSI = 7. RUSTLING
Soft fluttering or crackling sounds

8. OUSVCII = 8. VICIOUS
Savage; evil; dangerous

9. IGNFINLG = 9. FLINGING
Casting aside; discarding

10. NSSOIONUUPCCI =10. INCONSPICUOUS
Not readily noticeable

11. NFFTEEEMIA =11. EFFEMINATE
Having qualities usually associated with females

12. VIITTCRAIOADY =12. RADIOACTIVITY
Spontaneous emission of radiation

13. AILUCEPR =13. PECULIAR
Odd

14. UGMS =14. SMUG
Self-satisfied; complacent

15. AEHLILFF =15. HALFLIFE
Time for half of nuclei to radioactively decay

Gamma Rays Vocabulary Juggle Letters 3

1. RSGGTREI = 1. _____
   Precipitates; causes to happen

2. ASMURTOIAN = 2. _____
   A place of convalescence from illness

3. RNEFTME = 3. _____
   To seethe; to be agitated

4. ROIIAPSSS = 4. _____
   A skin disease

5. PSASG = 5. _____
   Sharp breaths

6. INOUVLCSSON = 6. _____
   Intense involuntary muscular contractions

7. CDCEAAETTUN = 7. _____
   Stressed; accented

8. NSATTALPNR = 8. _____
   Uproot and replant

9. EYITHSLRAC = 9. _____
   Having excessive or uncontrollable emotion

10. CMALHCNEYLIA =10. _____
    Like a machine

11. RENYEITT =11. _____
    Continuance without beginning or end

12. ERSVUSY =12. _____
    Examines; looks at comprehensively

13. EGXTEINRGAGA =13. _____
    Enlarging, increasing beyond normal bounds

14. EXAEETPRSA =14. _____
    Make angry or impatient

15. OEUTISTELH =15. _____
    Outline or profile

Gamma Rays Vocabulary Juggle Letters 3 Answer Key

1. RSGGTREI = 1. TRIGGERS
Precipitates; causes to happen

2. ASMURTOIAN = 2. SANATORIUM
A place of convalescence from illness

3. RNEFTME = 3. FERMENT
To seethe; to be agitated

4. ROIIAPSSS = 4. PSORIASIS
A skin disease

5. PSASG = 5. GASPS
Sharp breaths

6. INOUVLCSSON = 6. CONVULSIONS
Intense involuntary muscular contractions

7. CDCEAAETTUN = 7. ACCENTUATED
Stressed; accented

8. NSATTALPNR = 8. TRANSPLANT
Uproot and replant

9. EYITHSLRAC = 9. HYSTERICAL
Having excessive or uncontrollable emotion

10. CMALHCNEYLIA = 10. MECHANICALLY
Like a machine

11. RENYEITT = 11. ETERNITY
Continuance without beginning or end

12. ERSVUSY = 12. SURVEYS
Examines; looks at comprehensively

13. EGXTEINRGAGA = 13. EXAGGERATING
Enlarging, increasing beyond normal bounds

14. EXAEETPRSA = 14. EXASPERATE
Make angry or impatient

15. OEUTISTELH = 15. SILHOUETTE
Outline or profile

Gamma Rays Vocabulary Juggle Letters 4

1. TUACLEASCL = 1. _____
   Computes mathematically

2. SBVIAERT = 2. _____
   Shakes or trembles

3. NEISRSTI = 3. _____
   Threatening evil

4. RAVLIMPE = 4. _____
   Belonging to the first or earliest age or ages

5. HEUEITLOST = 5. _____
   Outline or profile

6. ESITNEBMTGO = 6. _____
   Of dubious origins

7. ASUCUENTPT = 7. _____
   Emphasizes

8. ROBHOTMSIS = 8. _____
   Blood clot in blood vessel or heart

9. CIUIVOS = 9. _____
   Savage; evil; dangerous

10. MBLTREE =10. _____
    Shake violently

11. PRIVGEPDOASNE =11. _____
    Listening secretly

12. TMAO =12. _____
    Smallest unit of an element

13. TECYSSA =13. _____
    Intense joy or delight

14. OCSMNMEEC =14. _____
    Starts

15. SREEBRK =15. _____
    Deranged; crazed

Gamma Rays Vocabulary Juggle Letters 4 Answer Key

1. TUACLEASCL = 1. CALCULATES
Computes mathematically

2. SBVIAERT = 2. VIBRATES
Shakes or trembles

3. NEISRSTI = 3. SINISTER
Threatening evil

4. RAVLIMPE = 4. PRIMEVAL
Belonging to the first or earliest age or ages

5. HEUEITLOST = 5. SILHOUETTE
Outline or profile

6. ESITNEBMTGO = 6. MISBEGOTTEN
Of dubious origins

7. ASUCUENTPT = 7. PUNCTUATES
Emphasizes

8. ROBHOTMSIS = 8. THROMBOSIS
Blood clot in blood vessel or heart

9. CIUIVOS = 9. VICIOUS
Savage; evil; dangerous

10. MBLTREE = 10. TREMBLE
Shake violently

11. PRIVGEPDOASNE = 11. EAVESDROPPING
Listening secretly

12. TMAO = 12. ATOM
Smallest unit of an element

13. TECYSSA = 13. ECSTASY
Intense joy or delight

14. OCSMNMEEC = 14. COMMENCES
Starts

15. SREEBRK = 15. BERSERK
Deranged; crazed

ACCENTUATED	Stressed; accented
ANATOMY	Structure of an organism or organ
ANCIENT	Very old
ATOM	Smallest unit of an element
BERSERK	Deranged; crazed
BOGEYMAN	A terrifying presence; hobgoblin

CALCULATES	Computes mathematically
CATARACTS	Opacities of the eye lens or capsule
CHLOROFORM	Chemical to anesthetize or kill
COMMENCES	Starts
COMPETITION	Others capable of winning
CONVULSIONS	Intense involuntary muscular contractions

COOT	An eccentric person
EAVESDROPPING	Listening secretly
ECSTASY	Intense joy or delight
EFFEMINATE	Having qualities usually associated with females
ETERNITY	Continuance without beginning or end
EXAGGERATING	Enlarging, increasing beyond normal bounds

EXASPERATE	Make angry or impatient
FERMENT	To seethe; to be agitated
FLINGING	Casting aside; discarding
GASPS	Sharp breaths
HALFLIFE	Time for half of nuclei to radioactively decay
HORRIFIES	Scares; shocks; causes horror

HYSTERICAL	Having excessive or uncontrollable emotion
INCONSPICUOUS	Not readily noticeable
JEALOUS	Envious
LOON	One who is crazy or simple-minded
MECHANICALLY	Like a machine
MIMEOGRAPHED	Copies

MISBEGOTTEN	Of dubious origins
MUTATION	A change, as in nature, form, or quality
NERVE	Brazen boldness
OBLIVIOUS	Unaware of
PATHETIC	Arousing sympathy and compassion
PECULIAR	Odd

PERVADES	Spreads throughout
PRIMEVAL	Belonging to the first or earliest age or ages
PSORIASIS	A skin disease
PUNCTUATES	Emphasizes
RADIOACTIVITY	Spontaneous emission of radiation
RUMMAGES	Makes a disorderly search of

RUSTLING	Soft fluttering or crackling sounds
SACCHARINE	Sweet
SANATORIUM	A place of convalescence from illness
SHUFFLING	Sliding feet along the floor
SILHOUETTE	Outline or profile
SINISTER	Threatening evil

SMUG	Self-satisfied; complacent
SNOOP	One who pries secretly
STAGGERING	Overwhelming
STERILITY	Incapability of producing offspring
SUFFOCATE	Kill by preventing access to oxygen
SURVEYS	Examines; looks at comprehensively

THROMBOSIS	Blood clot in blood vessel or heart
TRANSPLANT	Uproot and replant
TREMBLE	Shake violently
TRIGGERS	Precipitates; causes to happen
VIBRATES	Shakes or trembles
VICIOUS	Savage; evil; dangerous

Gamma Rays Vocabulary

CATARACTS	SILHOUETTE	MUTATION	VICIOUS	COMMENCES
TRANSPLANT	LOON	PERVADES	PSORIASIS	MISBEGOTTEN
PECULIAR	SHUFFLING	FREE SPACE	OBLIVIOUS	THROMBOSIS
TRIGGERS	COOT	SINISTER	PRIMEVAL	ETERNITY
NERVE	ANATOMY	SANATORIUM	EAVESDROPPING	ECSTASY

Gamma Rays Vocabulary

BERSERK	GASPS	SACCHARINE	CHLOROFORM	RADIOACTIVITY
EXAGGERATING	ATOM	STAGGERING	PATHETIC	EXASPERATE
EFFEMINATE	FERMENT	FREE SPACE	VIBRATES	SNOOP
ANCIENT	FLINGING	STERILITY	RUMMAGES	TREMBLE
SMUG	MECHANICALLY	BOGEYMAN	COMPETITION	INCONSPICUOUS

Gamma Rays Vocabulary

FLINGING	STAGGERING	ANATOMY	CHLOROFORM	EXAGGERATING
TREMBLE	TRANSPLANT	STERILITY	HYSTERICAL	ECSTASY
PRIMEVAL	SUFFOCATE	FREE SPACE	CATARACTS	OBLIVIOUS
PERVADES	EXASPERATE	VIBRATES	RUMMAGES	CONVULSIONS
MUTATION	ACCENTUATED	PUNCTUATES	COMPETITION	ETERNITY

Gamma Rays Vocabulary

SILHOUETTE	THROMBOSIS	GASPS	PSORIASIS	INCONSPICUOUS
SHUFFLING	EFFEMINATE	EAVESDROPPING	ANCIENT	BERSERK
MECHANICALLY	SMUG	FREE SPACE	PECULIAR	NERVE
JEALOUS	RADIOACTIVITY	TRIGGERS	HORRIFIES	MISBEGOTTEN
COOT	PATHETIC	CALCULATES	SANATORIUM	COMMENCES

Gamma Rays Vocabulary

RADIOACTIVITY	BOGEYMAN	SANATORIUM	ACCENTUATED	SILHOUETTE
ECSTASY	COMMENCES	ANCIENT	FLINGING	ANATOMY
PERVADES	EXAGGERATING	FREE SPACE	THROMBOSIS	EFFEMINATE
PRIMEVAL	RUSTLING	ETERNITY	SMUG	FERMENT
HYSTERICAL	SNOOP	GASPS	CALCULATES	PSORIASIS

Gamma Rays Vocabulary

RUMMAGES	BERSERK	VICIOUS	MISBEGOTTEN	HALFLIFE
SINISTER	SHUFFLING	PECULIAR	CHLOROFORM	PUNCTUATES
SURVEYS	PATHETIC	FREE SPACE	INCONSPICUOUS	MIMEOGRAPHED
EXASPERATE	EAVESDROPPING	HORRIFIES	MUTATION	MECHANICALLY
COMPETITION	SACCHARINE	TREMBLE	STAGGERING	OBLIVIOUS

Gamma Rays Vocabulary

CALCULATES	OBLIVIOUS	PATHETIC	TRIGGERS	CATARACTS
EFFEMINATE	BOGEYMAN	JEALOUS	INCONSPICUOUS	FERMENT
PRIMEVAL	SILHOUETTE	FREE SPACE	NERVE	PUNCTUATES
ANATOMY	ATOM	SURVEYS	STERILITY	PERVADES
SANATORIUM	VIBRATES	SNOOP	ACCENTUATED	MECHANICALLY

Gamma Rays Vocabulary

ANCIENT	TREMBLE	RUMMAGES	MISBEGOTTEN	COOT
PSORIASIS	CHLOROFORM	SUFFOCATE	TRANSPLANT	SINISTER
MIMEOGRAPHED	RUSTLING	FREE SPACE	EAVESDROPPING	PECULIAR
EXASPERATE	COMMENCES	MUTATION	HORRIFIES	HALFLIFE
COMPETITION	GASPS	EXAGGERATING	STAGGERING	THROMBOSIS

Gamma Rays Vocabulary

TREMBLE	PUNCTUATES	SHUFFLING	ACCENTUATED	TRANSPLANT
INCONSPICUOUS	CHLOROFORM	HALFLIFE	SMUG	MIMEOGRAPHED
LOON	COMMENCES	FREE SPACE	SILHOUETTE	BERSERK
PSORIASIS	VICIOUS	MISBEGOTTEN	FERMENT	HYSTERICAL
ATOM	MUTATION	NERVE	PRIMEVAL	RADIOACTIVITY

Gamma Rays Vocabulary

ETERNITY	SURVEYS	PATHETIC	STAGGERING	JEALOUS
SNOOP	SACCHARINE	RUMMAGES	PECULIAR	CATARACTS
THROMBOSIS	CONVULSIONS	FREE SPACE	COMPETITION	ANCIENT
SINISTER	FLINGING	TRIGGERS	BOGEYMAN	VIBRATES
EFFEMINATE	EAVESDROPPING	CALCULATES	GASPS	RUSTLING

Gamma Rays Vocabulary

PUNCTUATES	RUMMAGES	OBLIVIOUS	EXASPERATE	EXAGGERATING
HORRIFIES	RADIOACTIVITY	SACCHARINE	CHLOROFORM	CALCULATES
STAGGERING	ANATOMY	FREE SPACE	HALFLIFE	FLINGING
SMUG	THROMBOSIS	STERILITY	PRIMEVAL	BERSERK
SINISTER	ATOM	EAVESDROPPING	SNOOP	PSORIASIS

Gamma Rays Vocabulary

VICIOUS	COMMENCES	JEALOUS	TRIGGERS	LOON
INCONSPICUOUS	TRANSPLANT	ANCIENT	SHUFFLING	SURVEYS
ACCENTUATED	TREMBLE	FREE SPACE	RUSTLING	MECHANICALLY
COOT	COMPETITION	MISBEGOTTEN	VIBRATES	MIMEOGRAPHED
SILHOUETTE	CONVULSIONS	MUTATION	HYSTERICAL	BOGEYMAN

Gamma Rays Vocabulary

VIBRATES	TREMBLE	VICIOUS	ETERNITY	SURVEYS
FLINGING	SMUG	SANATORIUM	STAGGERING	ACCENTUATED
GASPS	PERVADES	FREE SPACE	HYSTERICAL	SINISTER
MISBEGOTTEN	SHUFFLING	COMMENCES	CALCULATES	NERVE
MIMEOGRAPHED	TRANSPLANT	CONVULSIONS	MUTATION	FERMENT

Gamma Rays Vocabulary

RUSTLING	EXASPERATE	COOT	BERSERK	EAVESDROPPING
CATARACTS	MECHANICALLY	CHLOROFORM	HALFLIFE	PECULIAR
TRIGGERS	HORRIFIES	FREE SPACE	ANATOMY	PATHETIC
ATOM	PUNCTUATES	ECSTASY	LOON	BOGEYMAN
SACCHARINE	COMPETITION	RUMMAGES	STERILITY	JEALOUS

Gamma Rays Vocabulary

SNOOP	JEALOUS	SACCHARINE	STAGGERING	FERMENT
ATOM	TREMBLE	RADIOACTIVITY	ACCENTUATED	SUFFOCATE
MECHANICALLY	EXAGGERATING	FREE SPACE	EAVESDROPPING	RUMMAGES
OBLIVIOUS	EXASPERATE	PSORIASIS	COMMENCES	INCONSPICUOUS
EFFEMINATE	BERSERK	VIBRATES	ANCIENT	COOT

Gamma Rays Vocabulary

FLINGING	HALFLIFE	TRANSPLANT	VICIOUS	SINISTER
CHLOROFORM	CONVULSIONS	ECSTASY	SMUG	PRIMEVAL
HORRIFIES	STERILITY	FREE SPACE	PERVADES	NERVE
ANATOMY	SHUFFLING	TRIGGERS	ETERNITY	HYSTERICAL
COMPETITION	MISBEGOTTEN	GASPS	MUTATION	PATHETIC

Gamma Rays Vocabulary

BERSERK	ANATOMY	ETERNITY	GASPS	RUMMAGES
OBLIVIOUS	PATHETIC	SNOOP	FERMENT	RUSTLING
LOON	MIMEOGRAPHED	FREE SPACE	VICIOUS	ATOM
SURVEYS	PECULIAR	SMUG	MISBEGOTTEN	BOGEYMAN
HORRIFIES	SANATORIUM	ANCIENT	TRIGGERS	THROMBOSIS

Gamma Rays Vocabulary

CALCULATES	PSORIASIS	RADIOACTIVITY	PERVADES	TRANSPLANT
INCONSPICUOUS	ECSTASY	EFFEMINATE	CONVULSIONS	STERILITY
EXASPERATE	NERVE	FREE SPACE	FLINGING	SACCHARINE
CATARACTS	VIBRATES	EXAGGERATING	COOT	MUTATION
HYSTERICAL	JEALOUS	MECHANICALLY	SILHOUETTE	ACCENTUATED

Gamma Rays Vocabulary

BOGEYMAN	SUFFOCATE	HORRIFIES	COOT	SMUG
MIMEOGRAPHED	EAVESDROPPING	FLINGING	TRANSPLANT	THROMBOSIS
SILHOUETTE	SINISTER	FREE SPACE	SACCHARINE	MECHANICALLY
PERVADES	STERILITY	VIBRATES	VICIOUS	GASPS
PSORIASIS	INCONSPICUOUS	MISBEGOTTEN	STAGGERING	CATARACTS

Gamma Rays Vocabulary

PUNCTUATES	RUSTLING	OBLIVIOUS	CHLOROFORM	RUMMAGES
MUTATION	SANATORIUM	TREMBLE	ETERNITY	PRIMEVAL
FERMENT	PECULIAR	FREE SPACE	SHUFFLING	ATOM
ANCIENT	EXAGGERATING	ANATOMY	COMMENCES	CALCULATES
EXASPERATE	ECSTASY	EFFEMINATE	CONVULSIONS	RADIOACTIVITY

Gamma Rays Vocabulary

SANATORIUM	ANCIENT	SHUFFLING	PATHETIC	NERVE
EXAGGERATING	TREMBLE	MISBEGOTTEN	ATOM	STAGGERING
MIMEOGRAPHED	BOGEYMAN	FREE SPACE	COOT	ACCENTUATED
TRANSPLANT	GASPS	SNOOP	STERILITY	EAVESDROPPING
VICIOUS	RUMMAGES	JEALOUS	MUTATION	CALCULATES

Gamma Rays Vocabulary

COMMENCES	EFFEMINATE	PERVADES	ANATOMY	MECHANICALLY
SILHOUETTE	CHLOROFORM	BERSERK	HORRIFIES	RUSTLING
SINISTER	THROMBOSIS	FREE SPACE	FLINGING	VIBRATES
CATARACTS	EXASPERATE	LOON	TRIGGERS	PRIMEVAL
OBLIVIOUS	COMPETITION	PSORIASIS	PECULIAR	SACCHARINE

Gamma Rays Vocabulary

TRANSPLANT	SUFFOCATE	EXASPERATE	COOT	PECULIAR
CALCULATES	ANCIENT	EFFEMINATE	OBLIVIOUS	MECHANICALLY
PSORIASIS	HYSTERICAL	FREE SPACE	SILHOUETTE	VIBRATES
HALFLIFE	LOON	COMPETITION	JEALOUS	STAGGERING
TREMBLE	EXAGGERATING	VICIOUS	PUNCTUATES	STERILITY

Gamma Rays Vocabulary

SNOOP	PRIMEVAL	SURVEYS	SINISTER	INCONSPICUOUS
PERVADES	MIMEOGRAPHED	EAVESDROPPING	PATHETIC	SMUG
TRIGGERS	NERVE	FREE SPACE	MISBEGOTTEN	THROMBOSIS
ANATOMY	COMMENCES	BOGEYMAN	RUSTLING	BERSERK
CONVULSIONS	SACCHARINE	SHUFFLING	FERMENT	ETERNITY

Gamma Rays Vocabulary

SURVEYS	BERSERK	THROMBOSIS	GASPS	COMMENCES
INCONSPICUOUS	CHLOROFORM	CALCULATES	EXAGGERATING	SHUFFLING
RUMMAGES	TREMBLE	FREE SPACE	MECHANICALLY	MISBEGOTTEN
SINISTER	FERMENT	JEALOUS	MUTATION	ETERNITY
TRANSPLANT	OBLIVIOUS	ANATOMY	PECULIAR	CONVULSIONS

Gamma Rays Vocabulary

HORRIFIES	RADIOACTIVITY	SANATORIUM	CATARACTS	ANCIENT
SILHOUETTE	LOON	PSORIASIS	NERVE	PUNCTUATES
ACCENTUATED	MIMEOGRAPHED	FREE SPACE	VIBRATES	ECSTASY
HYSTERICAL	STAGGERING	COMPETITION	PRIMEVAL	PATHETIC
EXASPERATE	SACCHARINE	VICIOUS	SMUG	EFFEMINATE

Gamma Rays Vocabulary

BERSERK	THROMBOSIS	EAVESDROPPING	STAGGERING	EXAGGERATING
RUMMAGES	FERMENT	PRIMEVAL	SHUFFLING	INCONSPICUOUS
ECSTASY	TRANSPLANT	FREE SPACE	OBLIVIOUS	HORRIFIES
SINISTER	EFFEMINATE	RUSTLING	NERVE	COMPETITION
PSORIASIS	ANATOMY	LOON	GASPS	TREMBLE

Gamma Rays Vocabulary

VICIOUS	PERVADES	HYSTERICAL	CHLOROFORM	COOT
CATARACTS	ACCENTUATED	MUTATION	MISBEGOTTEN	ANCIENT
ATOM	PATHETIC	FREE SPACE	JEALOUS	SNOOP
SILHOUETTE	COMMENCES	FLINGING	SUFFOCATE	MECHANICALLY
BOGEYMAN	SURVEYS	MIMEOGRAPHED	EXASPERATE	VIBRATES

Gamma Rays Vocabulary

ATOM	BERSERK	BOGEYMAN	CATARACTS	EAVESDROPPING
TREMBLE	MIMEOGRAPHED	SILHOUETTE	CALCULATES	COMPETITION
PERVADES	RADIOACTIVITY	FREE SPACE	VIBRATES	TRIGGERS
PUNCTUATES	OBLIVIOUS	ACCENTUATED	SUFFOCATE	MUTATION
PRIMEVAL	STERILITY	SNOOP	HALFLIFE	VICIOUS

Gamma Rays Vocabulary

RUSTLING	EXAGGERATING	SMUG	FLINGING	JEALOUS
PSORIASIS	GASPS	COOT	SANATORIUM	SHUFFLING
SACCHARINE	RUMMAGES	FREE SPACE	LOON	INCONSPICUOUS
PECULIAR	MISBEGOTTEN	FERMENT	ECSTASY	SURVEYS
NERVE	EXASPERATE	STAGGERING	ANCIENT	ANATOMY

Gamma Rays Vocabulary

HORRIFIES	CONVULSIONS	ANCIENT	ECSTASY	RUMMAGES
ATOM	COMMENCES	ACCENTUATED	PECULIAR	FLINGING
PRIMEVAL	PERVADES	FREE SPACE	THROMBOSIS	JEALOUS
ETERNITY	TRANSPLANT	SINISTER	INCONSPICUOUS	STERILITY
MIMEOGRAPHED	EXAGGERATING	MUTATION	ANATOMY	VICIOUS

Gamma Rays Vocabulary

FERMENT	SACCHARINE	SILHOUETTE	SMUG	SURVEYS
NERVE	STAGGERING	MECHANICALLY	RADIOACTIVITY	SNOOP
MISBEGOTTEN	EAVESDROPPING	FREE SPACE	PUNCTUATES	BERSERK
TREMBLE	OBLIVIOUS	GASPS	TRIGGERS	CATARACTS
EXASPERATE	HALFLIFE	SANATORIUM	SUFFOCATE	COMPETITION

www.ingramcontent.com/pod-product-compliance
Lightning Source LLC
Chambersburg PA
CBHW081455070526
44586CB00019B/2359